ISIS:
The Genetic Conception

LACK OF JUDGMENT

DR. JULIO ANTONIO DEL MÁRMOL

www.trafford.com
North America & international
toll-free: 1 888 232 4444 (USA & Canada)
fax: 812 355 4082

INTRODUCTION

Dr. Julio Antonio del Mármol, a freedom fighter and a master spy, has been identified by his enemies. His mission is too critical to abort, so he must deal with the immediate threat in order to be able to complete the objective given to him: to identify the new connections Cuba has to Islamic terror and to prove to his  friends in the intelligence community that it poses an immediate threat to United States security and the rest of the world.

Dodging Cuban counter espionage agents at every turn, del Mármol infiltrates the tightest security arrangements of the Cuban G-2 with the aid of fellow freedom fighters on the island, and is able to identify key agents from the Middle East. In the process, his mentor is also able to uncover a horrific assassination plot against the newly-elected President of Mexico and his entire family.

Despite the desperate urgency of his primary mission, del Mármol stops in Mexico to assist in averting the plot, while sending along the information he had just uncovered. Successful in his secondary mission, in addition to finding new love and making new important contacts, he is frustrated by the timidity of the bureaucracy controlling US intelligence. More proof is needed.

Del Mármol returns to Cuba to get the proof. As Dr. del Mármol discovers, the fanaticism of the jihadists creates an impenetrable wall, transforming into the most difficult job of his career: to persuade one of the radicals to cooperate with him in exchange for large quantities of money. He finally reaches an agreement with the terrorist to meet with one of his most trusted freedom fighters to close the final deal. Unfortunately, del Mármol is arrested en route to the meeting and has to escape from the police station. The delay scares the connection away, and so key information in preventing the planned attack is lost. Utterly frustrated, del Mármol is forced to leave hastily to avoid the massive manhunt mounted by the G-2 as they uncover his true identity as the most wanted spy, sought after for the last 40 years. Using a Spanish merchant ship to escape with the information he had been able to glean, he regrets missing the most critical piece of data, lost on the most random chance.

His enemies remain in hot pursuit, and ambush him in the United States. Though critically injured, is able to preserve the information his assailants sought. He is taken to a safe house in Mexico to recuperate. His recovery, however, delays further investigation, specifically in discovering the answers to precisely how and when the planned attack would occur. After brainstorming with his friends, the final keys are discovered, and they hastily depart for the United States to bring the information to his US contact. His assailants strike again as he attempts to cross the Mexican border, and have further designed another delaying tactic by arranging a security breach at the border crossing by having their own agents within US intelligence list him in the computers as "armed and dangerous."

Again, the bureaucracy moves too slowly, and by the time all the pieces are put together, it is too late to prevent the attack and the loss of thousands of innocent lives. All that can be done is to minimize the damage, rally the American people, and mourn the dead. Utterly frustrated, he leaves the country, realizing once more that the same freedoms he fights for also provide the greatest weaknesses for his enemies to exploit.

This story is based on true events. Some names, places, times and other details have been changed to protect the innocent.

In Memoriam

Maria Teresa del Mármol ("Beba") 10/11/1921-7/17/2015, and Alipio Rada Flores ("Cuco") 12/2/1928-1/18-2016

This book is dedicated to Beba and Cuco Rada, my aunt and uncle. I ask my Lord and God's Son, Jesus Christ, with all my heart to open the doors to Paradise for my favorite aunt and uncle that passed away recently. This is a mark of how much they loved each other, they died within six months of each other. They leave a deep, profoundly empty hole in my heart with their deaths. I will miss the immense love and generosity they always showed me without ever expecting anything in return. They consistently displayed integrity and unbelievable courage, never failing whenever I asked for their help throughout my life. I will never forget how, when everyone else showed reluctance to help, they offered, when I needed to abandon Cuba in that cold October night of 1971, to bring my car to my house from the train terminal. Had they not done so, it might have been discovered by the communist authorities and create an immediate manhunt for us, which might in turn have prevented our successful exit from the island. I always held debt of gratitude in my heart for them, one that could never be repaid. It is an example of the unconditional love that prompts us to offer aid to others, even at the risk of our own lives. To Beba del Mármol and Cuco Rada, with all my love and gratitude, I dedicate this small present, the first book in the series *ISIS: The Genetic Conception, Lack of Judgment*. I ask our Lord to bring them to His side in Heaven. They have deserved and earned this through their many exemplary acts during the time they were with us. We were all very proud to call them our family. As the defenders of freedom and moral principles and religious expression, these two warriors gave us the best of themselves as they leave behind beautiful and magnificent memories for all of us. Rest in peace, Beba del Mármol and Cuco Rada, in the Heaven you have properly earned.

Your Beloved Nephew,

Dr. Julio Antonio del Mármol

FOREWORD

The Character
of Dr. Julio Antonio del Mármol

My Open Declaration of the Exemplary Qualities of Dr. Julio Antonio del Marmol on the Day of My Centennial.

I am Dr. Hector Zayas-Bazan y Perdomo of the University of Havana, also known as "the Professor." For me it has been a great honor and a source of pride to be the political, intellectual, and ideological guides of Julio Antonio del Marmol from a very early age. From the moment we met, this young man cultivated my sympathy and trust through his extraordinary qualities. Over the years, I grew to love him as the son I never had and wished to have. His patriotism, courage, and high sense of honor are the most important of his qualities, as are his moral and religious values. While still extremely young, he proved to us his friends his extreme loyalty and his natural talent for leadership that without doubt he inherited from his great-grandfather, Major General Donato del Marmol y Tomayo, who fought to free Cuba during the Ten Years War against Spain,. A hundred years later, almost to the day, Julio Antonio del Marmol repeated history through his brave example to follow in the footsteps of his great ancestor. His path was slightly different and more complicated, taking him inside the strange machinery of espionage. He risked his life thousands of times in his noble effort to free Cuba. Over time, his task grew to become something perhaps a little more difficult and a more Gordian task: protecting the Americas and the world at large from the corruption and infiltration of the Marxist ideology.

Over the years, our relationship grew to be cordial and loving like a family, united working daily shoulder to shoulder towards the same goals and ideals of restoring freedom to Cuba. Dr. Julio Antonio del Marmol never stopped or had any hesitation or fear to put at risk his personal freedom or his life in defense of our cause and our fight to protect democracy, liberty, and religious freedom that the totalitarian regimes around the world indiscriminately attempt to rip out of our hands. That is why, in his great generosity, love of his fellow mam, and extreme dedication to our cause and our fellow fighters, this man has gambled his life repeatedly while defending the equilibrium to our democracies and freedom around the world.

I want to say very clearly on this my centennial in a very loud voice, yelling if necessary so that the world can hear me, that Dr. Julio Antonio del Marmol is not only a brave warrior and patriot like his great-grandfather, but also an extremely intelligent man. Julio Antonio is a true gentleman with a high standard of discipline and respect of the principles of our society, as well as being a humble follower of the only true king of the world and in the universe, the Lord Jesus Christ. That is why I, Dr. Hector Zayas-Bazan, live without any doubt in my mind that Dr. Julio Antonio del Marmol is the authentic new man, not the one the Communists have tried to sell to us. He is the original, not the imitation. That is why we should show him to future generations as the flag for our principles of democracy and freedom. All these many qualities I mentioned before prove to us through his life's trajectory an example for all of us, and fighting for God and liberty for all of mankind, all the while demonstrating a genuine respect for our brothers and sisters in the human race. His beautiful altruism, courage, and optimism are only possessed by the titans of mankind.

I write this letter as a corroboration of my deepest, profoundest thoughts that I sincerely profess for Dr. Julio Antonio del Marmol.

Letter of Reference from Dr. Hector Zayas-Bazan y Perdomo

Professor of University of Havana
Mentor of Dr. Julio Antonio del Mármol

A letter of reference on behalf of my great friend and brother in the battle to destroy evil in the world, the great master and teacher, Dr. Julio Antonio del Mármol

Early this afternoon, my team leader for over half a century offered me one of the greatest honors as well as one of the most difficult of my missions: describing him as a person and his values from my personal experience by his side for over fifty years. The most difficult of this particular target is that I only have one page to do this. I rolled my eyes and replied that I would try my best.

Let's begin by relating one of my many experiences by the side of this great, honorable man. Several years ago, after long hours in a semi-comatose state Dr. del Mármol recovered full consciousness. I looked at him with such great joy and admiration to see him come back to the world after fearing we had lost him. As I wiped the tears from my face, I smiled when the first words out of his mouth was to ask if everyone was OK—even in the midst of his pain and suffering, in such deplorable shape, with his face swollen to the point of deformity, and several broken bones. I told him, "Yes, we're all fine, and thank God you're still alive!"

With the determination so characteristic of him, he said, "Chopin, this ends right here and today. We cannot allow these people do to any one of you guys what they did to me, especially in our own backyard. We have to take off the white gloves of democracy and destroy once and for all these assassins, even if we all die in the process."

I wondered at the level of altruism, selflessness, integrity, and courage that has to possess a man who, even on the verge of death, can maintain his spirit at such a high level. He thought more of preventing what had happened to him from happening to any of us without worrying about his own suffering.

I can assure the readers of this letter that I would need several pages, perhaps even books like the one you now read, to describe in detail the qualities of my great friend and warrior, the one I have had the great honor of sharing many of his great adventures in an extremely modest way. I have no doubt in my mind that one day all the lies told by the extreme left wing will be exposed by the truth that Dr. del Mármol, lays before your eyes today.

Our enemies are your enemies. They bring the worst out of any human being, twisting great and noble men into miserable bandits and murderers. I ask you readers to listen to Dr. del Mármol and read all of his stories. It could be that one day he could come to be for you what he has been to this very day for me: my best friend and educator, both in politics and in morals. This man possesses extraordinary values incomparable to anyone I have ever met. His immense fountain of knowledge and intelligence makes me feel as if I had gone to every single university in the world and graduated with the highest honors. I conclude my letter in behalf of Dr. del Mármol, reaffirming with all my heart to all of you reading this that this man is the most dignified and noble individual that God has offered me the opportunity of knowing throughout all the time I've been living on this Earth.

"Chopin," Corona del Mar, CA, USA, January 24, 2016

This book, in my opinion, could easily be titled *The Naked Truth*. Dr. del Mármol told me once, way back before the terrorist attack on 9/11, something in his usual poetic fashion when he tried to convince me of his concerns that I have remembered ever since: "When a healthy tree loses its leaves outside the ordinary routine of the change in seasons, we have to look at the root of that tree to find the disease in order to cure the dying tree and at the same time prevent it from infecting all the other trees around it."

This is exactly what Dr. del Mármol presents us in his new book, *ISIS: the Genetic Conception—Lack of Judgment*. It is very difficult for us, growing up in this free society, to understand that so much of the vindictive evil related in this book is not the product of fiction from a novelist. Starting with my primary order from Dr. del Mármol, I can assure you as an active participant in many of the actions related in this story that he has a vast responsibility and the ability to maintain modesty by not exaggerating a single hair in this story. Of course, it's not necessary in this particular case, as he narrates the facts exactly as they occurred. I am an eyewitness on many occasions to the truth of this account. He has also meticulously subtracted from these narrations the precise methodology used by our intelligence agencies, and so has secured their present and future efficiency.

Now I move to my secondary order. I have known Dr. del Mármol for over four decades, and I can assure you with confidence and conviction that this man is alive only by extraordinary miracles, and there is no doubt in my mind that he still lives because our Lord has been behind him all this time. It is the only way I can explain the failure of multiple attempts our enemies have made against his life. It is with joy that I can say today that we have him still around us in 2016, with the same optimism, persistence, and hope that I have known from him all this time, from the day he stepped off one of our planes after being flown out of the Navy base in Guantanamo.

As I read these pages of this extraordinary story, I often grew frustrated by our sense of impotence, thinking what a pity it was that Dr. del Mármol had not been able to be more specific in some details. He would then convince the reader that his story is more accurately a depiction of real life than any other story written until now about the 9/11 attacks.

I have to contain an impulse to kick my own rear end because I was one of those who wound up being an instrument of terror. But my superiors and I had to maintain protocol, and our hands were completely tied. As I finished reading this book, I could not prevent tears of guilt from rolling down my cheeks as I recalled my own responsibility. I had not listened or acted on the urgent demands and suggestions of my best friend before this catastrophic terrorist attack happened. All I can say today is that this guilt and frustration I will carry with me on my conscience until the last day of my life.

As a member of the intelligence community for most of my life, I can assure you that the way Dr. del Mármol describes in this book is exactly how the events unfolded. I, O'Brien, strongly recommend that you not only read this book and recommend it to your family and friends, but also that you read all of the books that this extraordinary man writes and releases in the future. I assure you without any holding back, that we all, without exception—carpenters, mechanics, doctors, even the presidents of this country as well as other world leaders—have a lot to learn from the experiences of this amazing man.

"O'Brien," Newport Beach, CA, January 26, 2016

Silence Signifies Complicity

When we allow any government to abuse our freedoms in any way or form and we don't strongly protest, we contribute by our silence the destruction all our accomplishments and dreams. Without knowing it, we get in bed with the accomplices of the bullies who seek to repress us. We therefore allow them to build the most horrible and painful nightmare that anyone could ever imagine. Our cowardly silence makes us sit and contemplate the abuses committed against our freedoms, neighbors, families, and friends. Without our freedoms we lose our most valuable treasure, and so lose the greatest light in our hearts and our lives. The peace in our souls and the brightest dreams that men can ever have is our freedom; without it, we will not exist.

Dr. Julio Antonio del Mármol

PROLOGUE

Cuba, Pinar del Rio
The Town of Guane
September 1956

I was screaming in the bedroom in the middle of the night, soaked in sweat. I was around nine years of age. My mother tried to wake me up. I recall seeing her face fading in and out in the midst of this turmoil. They sat me up in my bed, and my father saw deep scratches on my chest and the back of my neck. Mima checked my temperature using her cheek against my forehead. She turned to my father and said, "My God, he's boiling with a fever."

My lovely black nanny, Majito, came into the room carrying a large container of cold water and some towels. She tried to assist my mother by drying my face and attempting to calm me down. Mima started to cry, asking, "God, why has this happened to my child? This is not the first time." She looked at my father. "What is wrong with him, Leonardo? What is wrong with him?"

Papi sat with a deeply concerned expression and tried to console her by touching her face. "Don't worry," he said. "I will call my brother." He stood up and walked out of the room. He soon returned with my uncle, an MD who specialized in pediatrics and obstetrics. He was a balding man with a very aristocratic demeanor, and he was dressed all in white. He examined me with a stethoscope. Then he noticed that the deep scratches went far down my back, even to where I could not reach. He shared a look of puzzlement with the others, but otherwise said nothing. My father had been watching and stood up. My uncle filled a syringe with medicine and injected it into my buttocks after Mima and Majito turned me over.

I saw his very disturbed manner as he spoke quietly with my father in the corner of the room, discussing my scratches. My father shook his head repeatedly. I was half-asleep, groggy from what I could only assume was a sedative that he had given me. I looked at Mima, who said, "Go to sleep, my love. You will have no more nightmares. I will be here to protect you."

As I grew groggier, everyone began to leave the room save for Majito, who stayed with me until I passed out. I later learned that my uncle had said to my father, "We have already performed every test we can do. This child is in as perfect health as one can expect. He's as strong as a bull, and you should be happy for that. My colleagues at the university concluded that this is something inexplicable. There is no logical reason for him to have scratches on his body in places that he cannot even reach. Even if he could, you guys have been very, very responsible to keep his nails trimmed and filed so that there is no possible way he could do that to himself. You may not believe what I'm about to tell you, my brother."

"Try me," Papi said. "I have complete trust and confidence in you. If anyone can help him, it's you."

"Scientists call this 'genetic link.' People who believe in the paranormal believe it is a spiritual connection between different generations." Mima and Majito were shocked by that statement, while my father shook his head in disbelief.

"For God's sake, my brother," he said, "don't tell me you believe in that witchcraft garbage. Do you know what you're saying, Emilio? Don't put things in Verena's mind—that's all I need! Please, she will take what you're saying very seriously."

My uncle smiled and shook his head. "Leonardo, my brother, you have to have an open mind. I'm a man of science. I don't believe in 'voodoo crap.' But science has its limitations. We have to keep an open mind and look ahead when we don't have answers for what your son is going through. We don't know what is creating those scratches. Normally, in an average child, nightmares and fevers disappear in the first years of their lives. Your son is about to turn nine, and this has been happening for a long time. We have no answers or way to respond to the symptoms. In my professional medical opinion, you should take him to a spiritual doctor to explore what science cannot explain."

Papi shook his head unhappily, but my uncle continued, "You know better than anyone that I am a doctor, and I don't believe in these things. But he is my nephew. Every time I see him like this, I have to sedate him, because I don't know what else to do for him. My heart breaks every time. Do you understand my frustration? Let these people try; my colleagues agree."

Papi said, "OK. Thank you very much, my brother." They embraced and exchanged kisses on the cheek.

The next morning, I woke up to see Papi, Mima, and Majito looking at me. It was a beautiful day in September. Mima said, "Good morning," as she gave me a hug. "Do you remember what happened last night?"

"No," I replied with a shake of my head. "What happened?"

"Don't worry about it. Go and have breakfast. You have to go somewhere." Mima checked my temperature. "He doesn't have a fever anymore." They all smiled in pleasure at that announcement.

Papi said, "I'm not going. You take him with Majito and see what you can find out."

Mima nodded and said, "OK. Thank you." She turned to Majito. "We will go and see Gojita."

Majito's eyes widened. "My lady, you don't have any fear? Some people say she is a witch."

I jumped out of bed with more energy than ever. "No, Majito, that's not true. My friend told me she cured his father from pain in his neck and headaches that he'd been suffering from for years.

Many doctors had tried to cure him and failed. If she cured Alfredo's father, she must be a good person. She cannot be a witch."

Mima smiled and looked at me in admiration for my reasoning. She asked me, "Who do you take after to be so smart?"

I looked at her and said, "I take after my Mima and Papi."

She leaned down and kissed me with a gentle laugh. "OK, let's get ready. I'm going to go get dressed." Majito remained in the room to get my clothes ready.

Once everyone left the room, I said to her, "Can I tell you a secret?"

She looked at me. "Of course, my son. You know you can tell me anything, and I will tell no one else."

"Are you sure? Not even Mima and Papi?"

"Of course."

"Well, Mima asked me if I remembered anything about last night. I told her I didn't remember much of anything, but that's not really all true."

"Why is that?"

"I remember some."

Majito sat down on the bed and put her hand on my head. "Sit down with me and tell me."

"I had a vision. I saw my little brother, Nando, playing on his tricycle in the driveway. A salesman that comes all the time to Papi was saying goodbye to everybody and leaving. He didn't see that Nando was behind his car, and so he got into his car and put it in reverse. He ran right over Nando. Nando died, but Mima brought him back by pushing on his chest several times. When everyone was crying, thinking he was dead, he came back to life. I saw him dead, and that is why I screamed and cried."

"Why didn't you tell your parents that?" she asked.

"I was afraid," I replied. "I was afraid they were going to think it was me who brought that on him."

After we were dressed, Mima, Majito, and I visited the small *bohío* that belonged to Gojita. The thatched hut built of palm trees was in the middle of nowhere in a very poor, rundown area. Gojita was an old West Indian woman with a lot of wrinkles on her face. She dressed all in white, including a white turban. Gojita greeted us with a big smile, revealing that she was missing some of her front teeth. After smoking a cigar and lighting some incense before a strange altar, she laid her hands on me. The whole experience was very scary, and my fear must have been evident.

As she touched me, her eyes widened in astonishment. "This boy is very strong, probably stronger even than I am," she said. "He is attached to a spirit—I think that of his great-grandfather."

She was speaking of my father's grandfather, Major General Donato Mármol Tamayo.

"Whenever he is in danger or whenever a major threat faces others," Gojita continued, "he will have these nightmares. The spirit scratches him in order to call his attention to the impending menace. He will never be afraid, so long as he learns how to use this gift."

She pled with my mother repeatedly to bring me back so that she could teach me to channel these good energies, enabling me to help a lot of people. Mima politely declined, explaining, "His father is a Mason. It was hard enough to get his consent to bring him here today. There is no doubt that he would never permit me to bring him back again."

Gojita shook her head in discontented disappointment. "What a pity. That is the only way this child will understand and use this precious gift he carries within him."

Mima assured her that she would at least try to bring my father around. They embraced, said goodbye, and we left. Although we would never again return, that conversation became indelibly imprinted in my memory for the rest of my life.

Only a few days later, on a sunny afternoon, I walked out of the house to see with shock and horror the picture of my nightmare repeat itself, exactly as I had seen before. I tearfully saw my brother's mangled body pulled out from under the car of the salesman as my mother administered CPR to bring him back. I crossed myself and silently thanked God for saving the life of my brother.

Cuba, Pinar del Rio
The Town of Portales de Guane
The Tobacco Farm of My Maternal Grandparents, Lorenza and José Barrios
Christmas, 1956
2:30 p.m.

All of my family were together around a huge table in the backyard of the farmhouse, celebrating Christmas in 1956. It was our annual custom. All of my uncles and cousins on both sides of my family got together, forgetting about the crazy times we were living in back then with all the violence and terrorism that surrounded the Cuban Revolution.

Every day the local police in every town and city had encounters with the rebels who sought to depose the Batista regime. The revolutionaries in their fight for power confronted the authorities as the students protested, demanding free elections. The primary leaders on both sides were not taking into consideration the safety or wellbeing of the common people. The two main forces against the regime were the 26th of July Movement, founded by the Castro brothers, and the 13th of March Movement, founded by the university students in Havana and led by the intensely popular and beloved José Antonio Echeverria.

These two opposition groups used the most grotesque methods of violent terrorism ever seen by modern civilization against their common enemy. They forced the dictator's army and police to overcome the insurrection movements by surpassing these methods in their quest to suffocate and destroy them. This only made the government forces even more repudiated by the people.

As they implemented more torture and repression against their opposition, they consequently failed in their objective. They naturally arrested innocent people on the charge of being rebels, and applied the same methods they used on the others. In reaction, the majority of the youth were pushed towards the opposition, seeking protection against the injustice and abuse of which they were victims. Even though they were only looking for peace and equilibrium, they were compelled by this dire necessity to choose the wrong side.

On this Christmas Day, we were sitting around the long tables in the *marañon*[1] orchard beneath the trees, eating, laughing, and having fun. My aunts and Mima brought in platters of pork chops, ribs, yucca, black beans—all the typical foods Cubans use in their Christmas celebration. Two large 55-gallon tanks, cut in half, were filled with ice and held bottles of beer and soda. The ice by now was half-melted, and so those who plunged a hand into the cold water pulled out bottles which were immediately sweaty.

My father's family sat around one table, my mother's at the other. The class difference between the two families was obvious. Mima's family were country people of humble origins without much education. Even though they were wearing their best clothes for this celebration, they were not of the latest fashion and bespoke strongly of the country. Even at the age of nine, they looked to me a little unpolished, and the distinction was tremendously obvious. Papi's family were all professionals – attorneys, university professors, and doctors. Even his sisters were high school teachers. Although they had dressed modestly for the country, they had an aristocratic air about them. However, both sides of the family ignored the differences in perfect love and harmony under the tropical sun in the comfortable temperature of 65 degrees Fahrenheit as they celebrated the beautiful birth of Jesus Christ.

That harmony flowed through both families until one of Mima's older brothers, my Uncle Pablo, the skinniest and most beloved of us all due to his personality, asked my father a question. "Leonardo, do you really think these bearded men can win the fight against the dictator?"

---

[1] Cashew apple

Mima raised her eyebrows, not liking the subject being introduced at all and clearly uncomfortable about it. Before he could answer, she said to her brother, "You should not talk about politics here, Pablo. Why are you pinching[2] Leonardo?"

She pointed to the table resplendent with food and continued, "Let me make clear before I say anything that I don't sympathize with the dictator in any way. On the contrary, I think he's an assassin, a thief who has stripped the Cuban people of their right to vote. Because no bad deed goes unpunished. They might manage to bring him down. But before Leonardo says anything, I want to let you guys know that if that is the case, we can forget about all of these celebrations, especially Christmas and remembering the birth of Jesus Christ. The communists are atheists. There is no doubt. They will try to strip us of all our customs and traditions, destroying our economy in the process. They won't leave anything for us to celebrate—not Christmas, not a single holiday, save for the ones they themselves create. Mark my words, this remedy will be a lot worse than the disease." She crossed herself. "Only someone completely ignorant can sympathize with what is obvious in these bearded men, but time will be my witness."

Everyone at both tables applauded Mima's speech, including me. I looked at my father out of the corner of my eye. He was clearly unhappy with what she had just said and was the only one not applauding. He smirked as he shook his head. He put his fork by his plate and said, "Pablo, as you all see, my wife won't let me talk but speaks on my behalf. But it's OK, because we do everything together. We're always one person; whatever she does is OK with me, and whatever I do is all right with her. I'll give you my answer. I believe strongly in my heart that we will win the Revolution. Not only will we win, but we'll clean our country and our social establishment, once and for all, of the injustice and corruption we've suffered for so many years. Even though I love Mima with all my heart – this woman is the mother of my kids and my lovely companion for many years—I don't know who in our

---

2   Egging on

family put in her head the idea that the rebels are communists. It's not only completely erroneous, it's misinformed."

He put his hand on Mima's shoulder. "You have to remember – what do women know about politics?"

That did not sit well with Mima, who rolled her eyes.

"This is not a communist revolution, and all those who think like Mima will have a big surprise," he went on. "In reality, no one in this country wants a totalitarian regime, and that's what communists are. Our revolution is a white and pure democratic one. No one will ever get away with trying to dress it in red."

Everyone applauded my father this time, perhaps to maintain the cordiality within the family—everyone, that is, except for my physician uncle, Emilio. He remained very serious and took it as a personal attack for having put the notion of communism into Mima's mind.

I was sitting next to him. He had no son, only a daughter, and he had a particular fondness for me. The whole family thought I was identical to his grandfather, Donato Mármol Tamayo, both physically and in personality. Emilio would take me everywhere with him whenever he came to visit.

He raised his arm to speak, a fork still in his hand. His smile was classy and his tone very respectful when he spoke. Uncle Emilio always displayed great manners to all. He said, "My brother Leonardo, with all my respect to your political ideas and your utopian illusions, my question to you is how you can assure yourself or anyone else what card these men in the Revolution bring up their sleeves? The leaders of this 'beautiful' revolution might have different ideas of which you're unaware, and their intentions can be so deeply buried in their minds that they won't reveal them to anyone until they are in power. They won't display these things in public until they know for certain they no longer need that public's support to get and maintain that power. Many good-intentioned people like you support these people because they don't possess the privilege to know as I do from the highest sources that these players are not only professional gamblers but are also at the level of magicians. They show you a rabbit, but before they make it disappear before your eyes have many other rabbits hidden away. The magician knows the rabbit won't survive the act, but he tells his audience the rabbit will be unharmed, will live a long life in great happiness and security."

He pointed the fork at my father, who was respectfully giving him his undivided attention. "My lovely brother Leonardo, communists and Marxists, like the Nazis and all other radical extremists, will never tell you their true intentions. They nurture themselves from the discontent and suffering of the ignorance of honest men of good will, such as yourself, to solidify and cement the terrible, bloody oppression of the system they intend to impose on the people. It has been shown and proved by history and the trail they leave behind wherever they put their filthy boots."

He put his fork down next to his plate and adjusted his sunglasses. "Unfortunately, ignorance is there. Be very careful, my brother Leonardo, and listen to your wife, because you could be an innocent victim and one of the useful fools that they will discard later once they no longer need you. That is the reason I left politics many years ago, because of the filth and dishonesty. It's not just that; it's also vindictive and murderous."

My father had stopped eating during this speech. He rested his elbows on the table as he templed his fingers. I could tell by his reddened face and ears that he was extremely irritated. He patiently listened without saying a single word until his brother had finished. That might have contributed to his blood pressure going through the roof.

Like a lion waiting in the grass to pounce on its prey, my father scratched his chin after a few seconds of silence. Finally, he said, "My lovely brother Emilio, if you know so much about politics to consider those who don't think like you to be 'ignorant and useful fools,' you might not have had so many deceptions and headaches during your political career. Evidently, all your political knowledge and savvy failed, because you gave your family a very difficult time. You not only put your security at risk for your political ambitions and the glory of being the mayor, but you nearly lost your life when someone attempted to kill you and your family. You can see that your erroneous political position nearly caused their deaths and nearly caused your wife to divorce you.

"Maybe, after all, I'm not on the wrong side this time with the Revolution. Maybe, after all, I'm not such an 'ignorant, useful fool,' and maybe, after all, the only ignorant person in politics after today, is you, my lovely brother Emilio." He paused. "My lovely brother Emilio, I would appreciate it if you would not judge my political ideas simply because they are in conflict with those of your friends and allies, whose only goal is to line their own pockets rather than to do anything noble or great for this country in all their time behind the scenes."

I glanced at my Uncle Emilio's face, which had turned red. I looked at my father fearfully, concerned that there was about to be more than talk going on here. Emilio looked at my father, not with hatred, but with a pitying, sad look of regret. He shook his head and smiled with all the politeness he could muster. He pushed his full plate away from himself in an apparent loss of appetite due to his disagreement with my father. He put his arm over my shoulder. Seeing that my plate was empty, he asked, "How about you come with me and we go for an ice cream to cool ourselves off?"

I smiled and said, "Sure." I raised my arm to get Mima's attention and got her permission. We left the table and headed towards his car.

Mima left my father's side and came after us. In a conciliatory voice, she said, "Please, Emilio, forgive Leonardo. He is completely blind with this revolution. He didn't mean to offend you; you know he loves you. I cannot understand what these people have done to him, because he has never been a fanatic, not even for sports. He's never voted his entire life for any political party."

She walked with us to the car, continuing to apologize for my father. Emilio put his arm over her shoulder. "Don't worry about it, Verena. I know my brother is a good man. When these bearded men betray him, they will break his heart with a disappointment so bad he cannot even imagine it."

Mima's eyes clouded with tears as she replied with genuine sorrow, "I know, I know. With anyone else, I'm not surprised. But from *Leonardo*, such an intelligent man. He's sending his money and that of all his friends—boxes and boxes of funds each month. Never before have we had even the most minor disagreement about anything; now we actually argue on nearly a daily basis as he tries to defend these people."

My uncle shook his head and grimaced. In a sad voice, he said, "Verena, don't give it up. Continue your political education, and maybe we'll be lucky one day and see him wake up."

Mima replied, "I hope it won't be too late."

Emilio's smile this time was forced. "It's never too late when the fruit is good."

He and I got in the car, and we drove along the dusty road by the farm into the little town. As we drove from the tobacco farm towards the highway, my uncle looked at me silently before asking, "What do you think about these bearded men and the Revolution in general?"

I glanced at him uncertainly before replying. "You won't be mad at me if what I say isn't what you want to hear, like you got mad at Papi?"

He did a double take at that. "I'm not mad at your Papi; he's angry with me."

I still wasn't very convinced by that. "That is the reason you didn't finish your plate and left that delicious food on the table? Come on, be honest—you guys are both mad at each other."

He gave me wondering smile. "OK, you're right. We're a little mad at each other."

I smiled back in satisfaction at hearing him admit that he had become angered. "I'll tell you the truth," I said. "I like the Revolution, like my Papi. Even though there's been a lot of death and sacrifice, in the end, like Papi says, it may be the last chance the Cuban people have of fixing all the injustice and abuses the current government commits against every citizen daily."

My uncle smiled in irony as he shook his head. "All these abuses you're talking about—no one's abused me or been unjust towards me. This government has only arrested those involved in terrorist activities. They put bombs everywhere, they're killing police, burning buildings, and doing crazy things like that." He scratched one of his ears. "Maybe the police are going a little overboard in their interrogations and in the way they treat these delinquents." He looked at me seriously. "I want to ask you a question: if you're one of the police and arresting one of those guys, and know that one of these guys killed one of your friends, would you not squeeze him hard to find out who had done that crime, out of the memory of your friend who had been killed?"

It made sense to me. I thought about that for a bit. I nodded slowly and said, "Yeah. Yeah, I would probably do the same."

My uncle smiled in satisfaction this time. He put a hand on my shoulder. "I always say to your father that you are the most intelligent of his sons. You know you're my favorite nephew."

I smiled sardonically. I looked into his eyes as I replied. "Why? Because I answered your question the way you expected?"

"Yes, of course, *claro*[3]! That told me that you will never be a puppet of anybody or a fanatic to any political doctrine. You use the most precious instinct that many men lack: common sense. Even scientists and highly educated men don't have common sense sometimes. It is a natural gift that gives you the opportunity to put yourself in the shoes of another person before you judge any act they might commit. That makes you different and gives you the quality of one day being a great leader."

My uncle lapsed into silence for a few seconds. By that point, we had reached the small town with the ice cream parlor. We could see the multicolored cones reaching up and the large sign proclaiming that it was the only ice cream establishment in the whole town.

As my uncle parked the car, I broke the silence and said in gratitude, "Thank you, and you're my favorite uncle, too. I wanted you to know that baseball is my favorite sport, and my favorite team is the Havana team. I'm not a fanatic or blind. When I watch the games, I can see our players make errors which sometimes cause us to lose the game." I shook my head. "But, no matter how upset I am, I still recognize that we made the mistakes. Even

---

[3] Clearly

though I respect Papi and don't want to contradict him, when our team loses, he tries to justify it and blame it on the umpire. Instead of getting upset with our team, he gets angry with the umpire and says they don't know the rules and are blind."

This time, my uncle grinned broadly. "Well, well—that is what makes you see things in life a lot more clearly, when you can recognize your own mistakes, even those of your own family." He opened his door, still smiling from ear to ear. "Let's go for those popsicles. We'll take some to your father. That way, he'll see that we're not resentful. That will be his dessert as well as for the rest of the family. As for what concerns me, I'm glad I left the food. Pork isn't that good for you, and I'll fill up the space with this delicious ice cream."

I smiled and got out of the car as well. We entered the parlor together. The attendant introduced herself as Gloria. She was a heavyset woman with red cheeks. She smiled pleasantly and said, "What can I do for you today?"

My uncle replied, "I'm going to eat ice cream until my heart is content and my blood pressure is lowered."

"Honey, you're in the right place! We have forty-seven flavors of ice cream and are proud to offer all the tropical fruits."

"My favorite one is coconut. Do you have that?"

"Yes, sir!" My uncle ordered twenty different flavors of ice cream covered in chocolate, and asked her to put them in coolers with dry ice. Then she asked him, "And what would you like now, since I don't think you're going to wait until you get home?"

"I want a *coco glace*[4]."

I chimed in, "I want that, too!"

While we waited for Gloria to get everything together for our order, we sat down at a small table next to the window so we could look outside as we enjoyed our *coco glace*. As we ate, we could see police cars starting to arrive with the secret police in civilian cars. They began to erect barricades in the street and stop the traffic. Before long, a line of cars had formed. They performed a thorough search, even of the trunks of people's cars. We weren't alarmed by

---

[4]   Coconut ice cream in a coconut shell

this, as it had become routine in the past year. The Revolution's forces had gained in strength and were consolidating their power, and terrorist acts had become common in both town and city. In reaction, Batista's forces had begun to frequently search the areas for signs of rebel activity.

We ate our ice cream and enjoyed the free show of people getting peacefully out of their cars. Gloria brought the box of ice cream to our table, and my uncle paid her. The search outside continued without any major incident until four men driving a 1953 mint green and white Chevrolet Impala suddenly pulled up. They sprang simultaneously out of the car and ran towards the vehicles of the police and secret police. They screamed, "Death to the tyrant! *Viva la revolución!*"

They were very young, perhaps not even twenty. They pulled the police out of their cars, and each one jumped into a different police car. The police and government agents were taken completely by surprise. Even though they had automatic weapons hanging from their necks, they had no time to even open fire. After a moment, they piled into the other cars. As they did so, however, four tremendous explosions in chain shook the entire town as each of the commandeered cars burst into flames. The concussion was so bad that the front half of the parlor's roof collapsed, sending the large sign and one of the cones down to the street, nearly missing my uncle's car as it crashed down.

We were both completely paralyzed in shocked surprise. I suddenly felt my uncle's hand grabbing me by the back of my neck and pulling me onto the floor behind the back of the booth in which we sat. At that moment, my uncle had realized that the Impala, in its position in the line of cars, was practically next to the ice cream parlor. The car exploded, and one of its doors flew through the air and crashed through the window of the shop— right where we had just been sitting. It appeared to me like a kite had just flown over us. It flew right through the store, into the back of the shop, cutting Gloria nearly in two. She didn't even have time to scream. Glass shards washed over us as we lay on the floor.

I raised my head a little bit, but all I could see was the blood flowing freely out of Gloria's mouth, her open, vacant eyes practically bulging out of their sockets. My uncle, seeing the expression of terror in my face and my eyes wide with panic, took my face in both his strong hands and forced me to look into his face.

"My son, my son," he said quietly, "go outside right now and wait for me in the car. Don't stare at this any longer. It's very depressing, and at your age it could create serious mental trauma. You are OK, and I'm OK, thanks be to God." He handed me the keys. "Now, go out to the car."

Gently but firmly, he helped me up and propelled me towards the door, pushing me outside. I looked at the floor near the booth we had been sitting in and where we had taken cover, and it was covered solidly in broken glass. I could not believe that I had come out of that without a single scratch anywhere on my body. I walked through the door checking myself for injuries. I was dazed, in a state of shock over what had just happened. As I passed by the ice cream counter, I could not help it. I glanced once more at Gloria and saw in revulsion her intestines hanging out over the door which had her pinned to the wall like a grotesque insect. My uncle was coming behind me to check on her, and waved me hurriedly on outside. She was convulsing and jerking slightly, and he needed to see if there was anything that could be done for her.

I did not want to disobey my uncle, so I rapidly left the shop and went straight over to the car. I had to make my way carefully, as I had to navigate the wreckage of the sign, and the electrical wires were still sparking and lashing around with current. I got into the car and looked into the parlor. I saw my uncle attempt to attend to Gloria. However, she didn't respond, and she soon stopped moving entirely as life left her body. She went completely limp as she gave her last breath, her arms hanging at an unnatural angle.

My uncle shook his head in frustration and crossed himself before washing his hands in the sink behind the counter. He walked back to the booth and picked up the box of ice cream we had purchased. He walked out of the parlor and towards the car, carefully avoiding the live wires.

When he opened the door, he said, "Poor woman. What a way to die. She was an innocent bystander. Just suddenly something flies through the window and kills her."

He noticed my unusual silence. "Are you OK?"

I looked at him seriously and nodded my head silently. He affectionately patted my head and started the car. Slowly navigating the wreckage in the parking lot which now resembled a war zone. The exploded cars were still on fire.

We returned to the tobacco farm. My uncle looked at me, still worried by my silence. "Are you okay? No need to be afraid. We're past it all, and we got away from that terrorist action, both of us without a single scratch."

He put his hand on the box of ice cream between us. "After all, I don't think now that it was a great idea to go have an ice cream. But who would ever think of that in such a small town in the middle of nowhere? I came from the capital all the way over here precisely to avoid all that stuff. What an irony! Today, there's no place where you can be secure. Wherever we go, these criminal terrorists follow us. These so-called revolutionaries, using as their excuse their desire to bring down the tyrant, kill innocent people like this woman without blinking their eyes. They couldn't care less about the suffering they inflict on the families of their victims."

This time, I nodded very firmly. Until that very day, I had never seen for myself the consequences of the actions taken by the revolutionaries over the past few years. I had only been hearing word of mouth from the people, because the government tried to hide all the bad news which would have a negative effect on public opinion. There was very little coverage in the news, whether on TV or radio, about all the bombings and the deaths of innocents that were occurring all over the island.

I looked at my uncle gravely for a few seconds and replied, "I don't have any fear."

He glanced at me. "Really? Why are you so silent, then?"

"Because I've been thinking, wondering how anybody could be so stupid to put a bomb on his own body when life is so beautiful. He doesn't take into consideration that life is a gift from God. Why destroy it in that absurd and violent way?"

My uncle smiled and nodded. "My nephew, unfortunately those kids who perpetrated that violent act are not as intelligent as you are. On the contrary, I assure you that you would never let anyone convince you to do this or brainwash you to die in that wasteful manner."

I nodded again. "Thank you. But I don't think you have to be very intelligent, not even a little. Just to have a sense of self-preservation and common sense."

My uncle smiled in satisfaction. "These terrorist methods aren't new, something invented by the Castro brothers. This has been copied from many religious and political extremists. They know their ideas are so far out there that the majority of people would never accept them. This is the only way they can take power: terror, intimidation, and coercion."

He looked away. "I just returned from Hungary, where the people of Budapest rebelled against the communist oppression of the Soviet puppets. They took to the streets in protest of all the years of abuse. Innocent, peaceful people were gunned down and run over by tanks, and the streets were filled with blood."

He shook his head and wiped his face with one hand as he remembered. "I cannot get that image out of my mind. Women took their children into the streets with them. No one expected that response. It was the most horrific thing I have ever witnessed. What the Marxist communists don't know is that with this criminal act, they have taken the first step towards their own destruction. They've shown the world what they really are and what they're capable of in order to preserve their criminal doctrine."

He leaned back a little to put his arm around me. "Believe me, my nephew, whatever your Papi says about this revolution and its leaders, he is completely blinded by the veil they've put over his eyes. He's fooling himself in exactly the same way as those kids who ended their lives so wastefully by blowing themselves up. The men who lead the Revolution are Marxist communists. The ones who aren't will wind up in jail with long prison terms or executed by firing squad. They will control Cuba and destroy our country if we don't do something about it—those of us who, as you observed, have common sense and see this coming."

I looked at him curiously. This was much different than what my father had repeatedly told me. Like an old man, I put my hand on my chin and shook my head in disagreement. "How is it possible that you are so convinced of what you say, when everyone else is saying something different? With all my respect, Uncle Emilio, I know you're an intelligent man and a doctor, but would you please explain it to me? I would love to find any logic in the basis of your theory." My look was imploring. I earnestly wanted proof so that I could believe him.

He looked at me with a flash of irritation. As though a cork had been released from a bottle, he shot back, "Because—" before he stopped himself. He pressed his lips together firmly, clearly biting something back.

He pulled over to the side of the road. He took some deep breaths as he shook his head. He put his right hand on top of my head and stared into my eyes. "You don't know how much pleasure it will give me to tell you what I have in my heart to convince you that what I'm saying is the truth. I have the facts to prove it. I don't have the smallest doubt that, in spite of your young age, you will be completely convinced, because you are so intelligent. You would believe not only that they are communists, but that they are also political delinquents. They won't just destroy our country; if we allow it, they will destroy the entire world."

He sighed and smiled at me ruefully. "Unfortunately, like I said, you are extremely young. There is a small possibility that your emotional state, a lack of maturity, or a lack of experience could lead to a small indiscretion and so expose the secret I would love with all my heart to reveal to you. The cost for me of any indiscretion would be too much."

I looked at him and smirked. "How much?"

"So much that maybe you could not ever live with it on your conscience." He drew his finger across his throat.

I leaned back in my seat, slightly in shock. He had never talked to me this way before. I gulped and took a few seconds to reply. "In that case, I would prefer to remain in ignorance of your secret."

He smiled in satisfaction and nodded. He put the car in gear and drove on towards the farm. "I don't expect less from you. You are, without doubt, very young, but with principles and integrity that many adult men lack. I don't have the smallest doubt of that. It says a lot of your character that you choose to protect my secret over satisfying your curiosity."

I shook my head and smiled a little. "My curiosity is not that important. For me, however, your security is. Thank you for your compliment, but I think you would do the same for me."

He couldn't hold himself in any longer and mussed my hair affectionately. We continued on in silence to bring the ice cream to our family.

Chapter 1

ISIS' CONCEPTION

Those that listen and follow any extreme ideas while blinding themselves with anger, hatred, and a lust for revenge for previous abuses that victimized them end up being the instruments, the useful fools, for the new and worse abusers. Before you know it, those tyrants gain power and control over your destiny by stripping you of all your rights.

Dr. Julio Antonio del Mármol

Norman Manley International Airport

1

Kingston, Jamaica
2000
11:22 am

I had spent the previous two years running all over the continent of Africa tracking several terrorist subjects and studying their movements. I patiently sat in a small corner of the airport, flipping through a magazine. My eyes, though, were everywhere. I was in a small salon waiting for the plane I was about to board for Cuba.

I was disguised as a mulatto Caribbean islander. My hair was tinted black and permed and I wore a prosthetic nose. My lips were also larger and thicker than normal for me. I was dressed in a black sport coat, white pants, and white shoes. My sunglasses appeared to be Calobars, but special crystals in the corners allowed me to see every movement behind me.

I turned slightly and saw behind me an old black lady in a wheelchair coming in my direction. Over the loudspeakers a female voice announced, "Flight 112 from Kingston to Havana departs in twenty minutes. Please approach Gate 6 for boarding."

I closed the magazine and leaned forward slightly in my chair. I opened my bag and put the magazine inside it. As I leaned back in preparation to stand up, I saw that the old lady was closer to me. She came up next to me and tapped my left leg with another magazine. I smiled and looked at her. The face looked familiar. With a small smile, she held the magazine out to me. I didn't take it, because she had not identified herself to me. Her smile faded, and she looked at me over the rims of her sunglasses, holding the magazine out in a more demanding way.

"On page eighteen, you will find an interesting article which says the Cuban government will hold free elections very soon." As she said those last words, she smiled cynically at the irony of the statement. I realized at that moment that the old lady was my friend Chopin, in near-perfect disguise. I smiled again, this time in relief, and I took the magazine without any more concern.

"Thank you very much, *lady*," I said with only the slightest emphasis on the last word.

In his own voice, Chopin whispered, "Don't be cute, eh? Don't get on that plane for any reason at all on Earth. Cuban intelligence is waiting for you at the Havana airport. They have a picture of you in this disguise. This information comes compliments of our Amazon in Varadero Beach. She sends you lovely, cordial regards. I will wait for you outside. Take whatever time is necessary. Be sure you check your tail, but do not get on that plane. They already have two men from Cuban intelligence who will escort you as soon you hit international airspace."

I twisted my head a little bit, and saw behind us two men who were watching us with a little too much attention. They looked like Cuban agents all right, in spite of their disguises. They also weren't getting in line to board the plane, which showed me that they were waiting to make certain I boarded the flight. My discomfort increased. I said to Chopin, "OK, lady." I lowered my voice to a whisper. "You can give me more details outside, OK? I think we've caught the attention of the two guys already observing us."

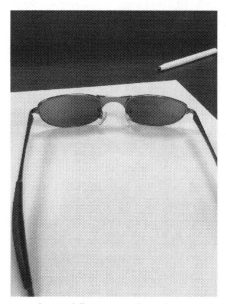

Special Rearview Sunglasses

Chopin nodded. He displayed a ten-dollar bill in his hand, and said loudly in his feminine voice, "Thank you, Massa. You are a good and generous man. God bless you for your great heart." I waved dismissively to 'her' with the magazine 'she' had just given me. I adjusted my travel bag, stood, and walked to the end of the boarding line. I kept the corner of my eyes on the two men. As I got into the line, I saw them rush to get into line a few people behind me. I opened the magazine and turned to page eighteen. There was a note with a paperclip attaching it to the page. It read in large red letters, *Great danger. Somebody has double-crossed us. Your cover has been exposed. Abort your mission. Tanya.* At the bottom, another message in black ink read, *Don't get on that plane in that disguise. We will wait for you outside.* There was a smiley face before and a cartoonish ghostly figure. It was signed, *Casper, the Friendly Ghost.* I grinned as I got out of the line.

I went over to a vendor that was selling *guarapo*[5] close to the boarding line. I ordered the largest glass possible so that it would take some time to prepare. I saw the men getting very nervous as they struggled to keep their eyes on me without losing their track. When I would rejoin the line, I would be behind them, and it would be difficult for them to make sure I got on the plane. As I waited and the line moved forward, the distance grew greater and their quandary increased.

After I obtained my beverage, I returned to the line. They looked at me and saw my appearance of casual inattention, sipping my juice through a straw. They calmed down at that sight. I kept my cover, remaining in line even after they had stepped through the door. I set my bag on the floor and fished around in it, waving people behind me on ahead. After doing this a second time, I was very glad I had used this stalling tactic. One of the men had conveniently 'forgotten' his carry-on bag, and was coming back from the plane to recover it. I could see his eyes looking all over for me.

I smiled and breathed a small sigh of satisfaction. I waited until the last passenger had boarded the plane. As soon as I saw

---

[5]   Sugar cane juice

they were about to close the gate doors, I headed towards the bathrooms. I went inside and cut up all the documents that tied me to that guise and flushed them into different toilets: passport, boarding passes, everything for that identity. After that, I put my carry-on bag on the long sink. I pulled out new clothing and accessories to change my disguise at once.

My hand still in the bag, I heard a voice behind me say, "Turn around very slowly with your hands up. Don't try any tricks. We've been studying you very carefully. If you want to continue breathing, do as I say. There are two ways we can do this."

Even though I was in front of the bathroom mirror, I kept my head down as if searching in the bag, my eyes locked on the corner of my glasses. My hand very carefully continued searching in the bag, but I kept my shoulders and elbows absolutely still, giving the impression that I'd frozen. I didn't want to prompt any overreaction or retaliation towards me. The men were behind me, silencers on their pistols, both covering me. I could see the determination in the eyes of both men. They would kill me without hesitation.

My hands discovered the two objects I was seeking: a cigarette lighter and a metal cigarette case. Cupping them carefully, I very slowly started to raise my hands as directed. To distract them, I raised my head and spoke to them with a smile, looking at them in the mirror before me. "My friends, I think you've got the wrong man. I'm a businessman. I'm on a trip to Cuba looking to increase my fortune. The only reason I'm here in the bathroom is that I'm looking for my cigarettes. I would rather miss the plane and catch the next one than leave here without my cigarettes."

The taller, more muscular one had the look of one from the lower classes. He yelled at the top of his lungs, "Fuck you! We know very well who you are and what you do! Cut out the bullshit—that's not going to get you out of this one!! Your luck runs out today. Slowly turn around if you want to continue in the world of the living. Let me make this clear: my orders are to take you alive, *if possible.*" He smiled cruelly. "They want to interrogate you. But if I can't because you resist or make it too difficult, they instructed me to cut off all your fingers for identification."

The other man was covering me, his gun in his right hand. His left reached into his pocket and pulled out the guillotine scissors used to trim the nails of very large dogs, and he clicked them suggestively. He smiled, showing his tobacco-stained teeth, and said, "If that's the way we have to do it, we'll do it with pleasure. I'll cut off your fingers and then we'll leave your body in the nearest trash bin in town. Our pleasure in doing this comes from the damage you've done to the Revolution and the Cuban people, motherfucker."

Still facing the mirror, I shivered exaggeratedly. "Oooh, that sounds violent and depressing," I said without any fear. I wanted to let them know they didn't intimidate me in the slightest. I grimaced as my jaw tightened, and I could not prevent my ears from reddening as I felt the blood rush to my face. Very slowly, taking great care not to let my emotions control my actions, I started to turn around, still smiling at them. I said to both of them, "Gentlemen, an intelligent man is the one who knows and recognizes when he's lost the game and is able to accept it. He prepares better then to win the next game. You got me. We should be brief and quick, or we'll miss our plane to Havana."

They both grinned ear to ear. The larger of the two said arrogantly in a satisfied tone, "My friend, I believe you've played your last game." With his free hand, he tapped the other man. "Cheo, come on—go and frisk him quickly. He's right about one thing: we'll miss the plane."

Cheo looked at him in astonishment. It was clear he didn't want to be the one to frisk me. He hesitated. His partner, noticing this, lost his concentration and looked at Cheo incredulously. Both guns were still trained on me, but neither man had his eyes on me. Cheo finally, reluctantly started to move towards me. This was my opportunity, and I pressed my finger down on the cigarette case. A poisoned dart shot noiselessly out and embedded itself in the right side of taller man's muscular neck. Instinctively, his gun hand raised up to touch the dart in his neck, but he was dead before he could do so. His last reflexive jerk caused the pistol to fire two shots into the ceiling.

Cheo had reached me and started to frisk me. He put the muzzle of his pistol on my chest when he heard his partner collapse. He yelled, "Don't move! What did you do to him?" He turned to look at him.

"Nothing," I said. "I don't know, maybe he had a heart attack. What do you mean?"

I dropped both the lighter and the cigarette case simultaneously. Both hit the tile floor with a loud, metallic crash, and Cheo snapped his gaze down and looked to both sides. That moment of distraction was all I needed to quickly snatch the gun out of his hand. He was about to say something, but I didn't let him finish. I shoved him back, and as he fell I shot him once in the chest and once in the head. I dragged both bodies and put them in the last stall in the line. I rapidly changed my disguise and left the airport in search of Chopin.

This time, I was the one who threw him off. He did not recognize me at once, since I was now dressed as an Arabian man in his mid-sixties and wearing a turban. I asked him, "Have you any spare change for cigarettes?"

He recognized my voice, and asked, "Did you get rid of your tail?"

"They are both out of circulation."

"Damn, so quickly? I wanted to be there to help you."

A few hours later, we left in a small Cessna piloted by Chopin, flying out of a small dirt field used by the planes that crop-dusted local farms. A little while later, we entered Cuban airspace on the occidental side of the island. During the trip, Chopin debriefed me on all the most recent developments that had nearly cost me my life and how he and the rest of the team had managed to intercept me in time to prevent it.

We continued our earlier plan, but now using an alternative method. I had the documents and IDs to support my new identity as an elderly Arabian man. We were going to obtain our enemy's latest secrets regarding international conspiracies inside the Cuban government with their ally al-Qaeda, led by their old associate, Osama bin Laden. Our information was that they intended to bring the U.S. government to its knees while at the same time striking panic into the free world through the most wide-ranging terrorist act in the history of humanity. Our objective was to obtain the information to not only destroy their criminal plans but also to know what kind of role the Cuban government was playing in it all. That was my specific mission.

Chopin flew in low to stay under radar. Even though it was the middle of a very dark night and we knew the current location of mobile anti-aircraft emplacements, thanks to our contacts inside government headquarters, our enemies also had small units with surface-to-air missiles which could spot us.

Everything went very well until we crossed an area in which anti-aircraft weapons appeared to have been more recently placed. They heard our engine, and powerful searchlights clicked on as they opened fire, spraying the air with flak. It was entirely due to Chopin's skill as a pilot that we were able to fly sideways through the barrage, bringing us through without any damage. It was only a few minutes, but the tension was such that it seemed to last much longer. We both crossed ourselves after we got out of that unexpected predicament.

I smiled as Chopin said sarcastically, "Thank you for that wonderful welcome, you sons of bitches."

I said, "You're good, man—you kept us alive."

A little while later, he alerted me to prepare myself, as we were approaching the area according to the map where I was supposed to jump: my family's old tobacco farm in Portales de Guane. I put my parachute on, made sure all the buckles were tightened, and picked up my bag with all the things I would need to survive. We exchanged a few final words before I jumped.

"Good luck, my friend," Chopin said. "Remember, I know you already have an exit secured, but if you need any help or need me in an emergency, page me. I'll be willing to land even in the Havana Malecón to get you safely back."

I laughed and gave him a thumbs up. He saw we were nearly there and gave me a countdown. When he reached zero, he gave me a thumbs up. I returned a military salute to him and jumped. A few minutes later, I soared over the tobacco bushes and landed on the farm. The peculiar smell of those raw tobacco leaves transported me back to years earlier, when I would play in between the plants with my cousins, ignoring the protests of my uncles and grandfather that we not destroy the field.

I noticed how many plants I had broken in my landing, and I felt incredibly guilty as I remembered how mad they had gotten when we had caused such damage. As I rolled up my parachute, I tried to right the plants, but many of them were already broken by my descent and simply flopped onto the other side.

As I finished wrapping up my parachute, I heard several dogs barking. The noise was getting closer, and as it had been many years since I had last been there, I took precautions. I left the parachute strategically concealed, and began to move away from the commotion at a jog. I used my compass to keep my orientation as I moved between the tall rows of plants. I needed to find the house where my uncle was to pick me up.

Family Tobacco Farm in Guane

The dogs were getting closer, so I sped up. I used my small flashlight to light the way ahead of me. I finally reached the boundary of the plantation. I could see the outline of the tall cashew apple trees. That silhouette brought many beautiful memories of my early childhood. I pointed my flashlight behind me. A few dogs were close—too close. Clearly, some had outrun the rest of the pack. I could see three brown and black Rottweilers. They looked like the dominant animals of the whole group and were about 100 to 150 feet behind me.

I pulled a pistol and silencer out of a concealment holster on my leg. I continued running as I screwed the silencer onto the muzzle of my gun. As I sprinted towards the trees, I asked God to give me the power and speed to get there before the dogs reached me. The last thing I wanted to do was shoot them, no matter who their owner might be. They were only protecting the property against intruders—which in this case was me.

I thought I could feel the leading dog's breath behind me as I reached the first tree in the orchard. I smiled and grabbed the lowest branch that looked like it could support me. I jumped in the air, climbing the trunk with my feet. One dog jumped and caught my right shoe in its mouth. I couldn't drag him up higher with me in the tree, as it was a very heavy animal. My left leg and hands were in the tree, my right leg dangling with the dog. I tried to shake it off me. I had to drop the gun so that I could hang onto the branch. As it dropped, it hit the dog squarely on its head.

It yelped in pain and let go of me. I pulled myself entirely into the tree, climbing as high as I could go. The other dogs arrived and jumped up towards me. I counted a total of eight dogs. My family had never had that many dogs before—perhaps only one or two. I was greatly concerned that I might have landed in the wrong location and grew worried. Doubts crowded my mind. Even if it were my family's land, perhaps the government had taken it away from them and given it to someone else, a family who would naturally be affiliated with the communist government. I could get caught by them after all.

My concern grew as I heard voices over the barking of the dogs. Powerful flashlights, like the kind used by the military, moved through the tobacco field, growing closer to me. I pointed my small flashlight down, looking for my pistol. It now lay on the ground beneath the paws of the barking dogs. I hesitated, thinking I might try to grab it in order to defend myself, but there was no way that was possible with so many dogs.

The lights drew closer, and the voices were clearer. To my relief and joy, I could hear the voices of my uncles Pablo and Emilio calling my name in hushed tones. "Julio Antonio, is it you? Please answer us."

They got to the dogs and pointed their flashlights up, locating me in my hiding place. I blocked the blinding ray from my eyes with one hand in an attempt to preserve my night vision, but I smiled at them. I waved my other hand, even though they might not be able to see it. I said, "Yes, it's me—I'm here. Don't get scared, because I don't look like myself. It's only a costume."

Uncle Pablo chained the dogs a short distance away. He smiled as I landed on the ground. "Where the hell did you get that nose?" he asked. "If you hadn't warned me, I would have gotten scared when I saw you. You look so ugly!"

"It's all fake," I replied, "but I have a better question for you: where the hell did you get so many dogs? I almost had to shoot them all to protect my life."

Pablo hushed the barking dogs by naming them one by one. The dogs were very obedient and quieted down. Then he replied to me, "Thanks to them, we are able to control the wave of thieves that is now Cuba. No one in the cities has food or clothes, and they come to steal our tobacco leaves when they're ripe to dry out and sell to tourists on the black market at government prices. Nobody wants to work in this country anymore—it's easier to simply steal from others. The government no longer provides anything to anybody."

I shook my head. "I believe you. This communist government has created a giant university for thieves, murderers, and terrorists."

We embraced and I looked at Uncle Emilio. He was much older than when I had last seen, still half-bald, but he had lost a lot of weight. I was a little taken aback at the difference in how he looked, and he returned the same surprised look at my disguise. He said, "Welcome to Cuba. Thanks be to God that you received our message in time. And thanks to your powerful gifts of persuasion in bringing Tanya to our side. She has become an asset of tremendous value to our cause. Since you saved her life, now it's been her time to return the favor."

I smiled and looked closely at him. With a slightly sarcastic expression, I replied, "Yeah, you're right, but we have to give some credit to her brother Ché. His desire for revenge was so extreme, he didn't hesitate when it came time to kill his own daughter. When he killed Maggie, he pushed Tanya away from him and anything related to the system he represented."

Pablo shook his head. "I cannot believe or understand how anybody could be so evil, but it shouldn't be a surprise. All these communists are identical, cut with scissors from the same cloth. They are like chameleons; it doesn't matter what you put them on, they always manage to change color to deceive you." The three of us laughed at his comparison.

Pablo said, "I know it's very late, but I would love for you to say hello to the rest of the family."

Uncle Emilio held up his hands and very gravely said, "No, no, no, Pablo—be serious. That cannot be. First of all, they won't recognize him like this. We can't reveal what we're doing, and I don't want anyone to see him wearing this disguise. We would not only put him at risk, but the whole family will be jeopardized as well. We can't let anyone know he was ever here."

"OK, OK," Pablo said, "but I wanted them to see him. It's been so long."

"Yes, but no one can know. And burn that parachute in the field. All the precautions we take now will be useful later. We cannot let our feelings interfere with what we're doing, and we can't afford to take any risk. All of our lives – his, yours, mine, the family's—will be in danger."

"OK, OK, OK," Pablo said in an attempt to stop the stream. "I'll do exactly as you say." He gave me a hug. "Well, *caray*[6], welcome and goodbye. God be with you, my nephew." He reached into his pockets and gave me a handful of cigars. I looked at him askance. He knew I didn't smoke. "Don't look so shocked. I saved these for you, because they must serve to bribe other communists who might want to give you some trouble on the way to the capital. You'll need all the help you can to reach there safely. You know how everything is rationed, and these parasites love to have some freebies."

I smiled and shook my head in admiration. "You always think of others. Thank you."

He said goodbye to Uncle Emilio and went towards the field to retrieve the parachute. Emilio and I headed into the storage house where his car was hidden. When we got to the car, Emilio shone the flashlight into my face. He asked me again with a worried expression, "Everything on your face is removable? Nothing is permanent?"

I smiled again. "Everything except my hair. It's actually mine, just dyed black and permed with the same chemicals they use in beauty salons."

He shook his head again. "You did all this yourself?"

"Yes, in less than half an hour."

"You've become a master of disguise!"

"I learned from two great teachers: you and the General. And I graduated from the master, Yaneba."

He scratched the side of his head above his ear. "The way you look right now, I don't think even Verena and my brother Leonardo would recognize you. By the way, how are they?"

"They're great, never better. My father's gained nearly twenty-five pounds. He loves the ham and the Coca-Cola."

"Who would have believed many years ago that he would be there in the U.S. and I would still be here? What a disappointment for your father all of this has been."

---

6   Damn it

"You don't even know. He cried like a baby on my shoulder when I picked him up at the airport. He could barely form the words to ask me for forgiveness. I think he'll die with the thorn in his heart of having helped these people. He still feels responsible for his actions."

"Yes, my God, I remember how blind he used to be," my uncle said. "He wouldn't talk to me for years following that Christmas argument we had." He turned the flashlight off, and we got into the car. He kept looking at me in the radiance of the dome light. He shook his head admiringly. "You have to tell me how you are able to so utterly change your features like that."

"The new technology," I said. "Prosthetics."

"Can I touch it?" he asked.

"Sure," I said.

He continued in awe, touching my nose. "You look like another person."

"That's the objective. That way, we can make our trip to Havana without any problems."

He started the car, and we drove along the dusty roads of the tobacco farm towards the main highway leading to the main provincial city of Pinar del Rio.

As we drove, I said, "If you please, when you see Tanya, give her my most sincere thanks."

He glanced at me with a small smile. "You'll probably be able to do it yourself. She'll be waiting for us, and tomorrow she is the one who will be with you, providing all the debriefing necessary for you guys to successfully pursue your mission. Hopefully you'll get whatever you need to expose their terrorist plans once and for all."

I smiled and replied, "I'll do as I always do: the impossible. The rest I will leave to the Lord."

My uncle patted my shoulder affectionately. "Why don't you lie back and rest? You must be tired. The night will end soon, and you have a hectic day ahead of you. I'll let you know when we reach the city."

"OK," I said. "Thank you. You're right. I'm completely exhausted. I've gone without sleep for several days tracking down these terrorists' leaders all over Africa."

My uncle looked at me compassionately. Observing my fatigue and the frustration on my face, he said, "This communist government has had four decades to export terrorists all over the world. They started in Algeria. Like vultures smelling rotten meat and knowing these African nations are poor and easy prey, they recruit the youth to bring here. They train them on our soil to later send back into the world like killer bees to invade honeycombs that they can control around the world. That's how they spread their miserable waves of terrorism and expand their reign over the rest of humanity."

He shook his head in a clear gesture of frustration, continuing, "And the erudite bureaucrats in our intelligence agencies unfortunately don't want to accept the reality that's before their eyes: that the only purpose of the Cuban government is to bring terrorism and destruction into the living rooms of every single home and hearth in the U.S.A. Of course, they use a pair of murderer's hands that is not publicly attached to them. They then avoid paying the price of their action or facing retaliation, because it doesn't appear that they are directly involved in these acts."

I adjusted my car seat back slightly and replied, "Well, that is one of the reasons I'm here now. You taught me that in order to uncover the criminal, I have to follow the money. That's what I've been doing. Right here is where the trail leads me. The money, evidently, has been coming from here. Maybe tomorrow we will obtain the proof, and in time we will finally be able to reveal and destroy these people's morbid intentions before hundreds if not thousands of innocents pay the price for our own negligence. Maybe this finally will make our intelligence community wake up from the sweet dreams in which they're living: that these terrorists will never dare to directly attack the United States. According to our intelligence forces, the terrorists fear the consequences that we would act on them if they did."

I scratched the back of my head. "I have to ask myself why the decision makers in our intelligence agencies think that these Muslim extremists are not going to be taking these terrorist acts to the rest of the world, including the U.S.A.? In the name of jihad, they blow up our embassies in Dar es Salaam and Nairobi. They repeat these attacks in Tanzania, Sudan, and other places. They have knowledge that terrorist leaders—Fazul Abdullah Mohammed, Abdullah Ahmed Abdullah, and other lieutenants we have positively identified—have been trained here in Cuba. They know these people are acting under the direct orders of bin Laden.

"To me, this is not only unbelievable, but it is arrogant, prima donna-like, and irresponsible. People will train, thinking this way. The people who direct our agencies supposedly have better training than we have. What can make these people believe that any terrorist at this point will be afraid of an act of retaliation when they've already committed these acts elsewhere in the world without any retaliation? This tells me we have a very serious problem."

My uncle replied, "My nephew, even though the roots of this tree began many years ago, I have to admit that under President Clinton's administration, it looks like it has accelerated. We should not blame our intelligence. We should blame the politicians in charge. The terrorists have been looking for the possibility of a lack of character, morality, values, and a strong hand in this leader, and they lack respect for him. They have no fear, and they have come to believe that, like the donkey in the game, they can hang the tail on our ass. They see the opportunity, and they're grabbing it. We cannot blame them; we gave them the chance to do this to us. That is obviously from our lack of judgment."

I reclined my seat all the way back. With a vague gesture of my left hand, I replied with a small smile, "Maybe, maybe." I recalled that my uncle never really cared who the president of the United States was, so long as it wasn't a member of the Democratic Party. That affiliation gave him more than sufficient reason to mistrust a president. He could never forget the old wound, still open after so many years, of the betrayal caused by the political maneuvers surrounding the Bay of Pigs by John F. Kennedy, the man who represented the party at that time.

His voice started to sound far away, and I fell into a deep sleep.

Dr. del Mármol c. 2000

Chapter 2

THE PRIMARY MISSION

A few hours later, I was awakened by a hand fishing a pair of cigars out of my shirt pocket. Still half asleep, I opened my eyes and saw my uncle looking into them. He smiled through the window of my door. He said very seriously in a soft voice, "Pretend that you're still asleep. I think I've got this. Don't worry."

That brought me to full alert, but I kept up the pretense. A short distance away I could see a pair of soldiers by a fire in the middle of the highway. It was the entrance to Pinar del Rio, and they were searching all the cars, trunks, and luggage. My uncle walked over to them, and handed each of them a cigar. They saluted and waved their thanks to him. He turned around and walked back to the car.

He turned the engine on and said in a low voice, "Continue to pretend to be asleep until we get out of here." I maintained the pretense until we had left the soldiers behind. "You can see your Uncle Pablo was right on the ball. Those cigars helped us get out of that situation. They didn't even search us. I don't know what you brought in that backpack, but I didn't think it would be any good for them to find something unusual in there."

"What happened?" I asked.

"The usual. They need to follow the protocol, and they wanted to go through your backpack. I told them that you had come from a foreign commission, and they had assigned me to bring you to visit the tobacco farms because of your interest in doing business in Cuba. I told them that on top of everything, you were asleep and that it wouldn't do to go through your stuff while you slept. When that didn't work, I told them I was with the Ministry of the Interior and that if they didn't comply, I would have to report them to the Minister, and they would wind up working in Angola. Finally, my closing point to clinch the deal is when I offered that if they ignored the rules in this special situation that I would give as a present a couple of those delicious cigars from the special reserve of Fidel."

I smiled. "The special reserve of Pablo, you mean? You just switched the names, right?" I raised my seat up. "You really have an ID from the Ministry of Interior?"

My uncle nodded. He smiled sarcastically as he pulled out an ID with a badge out of a black vinyl wallet, just like the G-2 possessed. "My nephew, here in Cuba, everything is possible with the right connections. How do you think I've survived all these years?"

I shook my head and smiled again. "I remember now. I almost forgot how you live in Cuba like a master *del puro cuento y el invento diario*[7]."

We looked at each other and burst out laughing.

A few hours later, daylight had broken, and we entered the city of Havana. A short while later, we reached a beautiful, private gated resort by the ocean that was exclusively used for tourists. My uncle identified himself at the security gate and pulled up outside a luxurious bungalow. Tanya came out with a big smile to receive us. She was older, but still beautiful. She held back a little when she saw me.

"Julio Antonio?" she asked tentatively.

"Yes," my uncle said.

"Oh, my God! What did you do to yourself? I had my doubts initially, but now I see no one will know who you are." She hugged

---

[7] Of bullshit and daily invention

19

me. "Thank God you got my message in time. I was worried sick, thinking you would come to that airport and leave as a dead man."

"I don't know if this counts as one more attempt," I said, "but I think we managed to detour the real attempt before it happened." She pushed me back. "Let me look at you. My God, what did you do to yourself? I hope you can go back to yourself when this is over."

"Don't worry," I assured her, "everything here is fake. The only real thing is underneath, where they cannot see."

My uncle, Tanya, and I spent long hours discussing the plan—not only how we would obtain the information we were looking for but, most important, how we were going to get it out of the conference without being discovered. We needed to cover all details in case an emergency exit became necessary. Around noon, we sat down at a round table and had room service. My uncle ordered a first-class lunch.

"We should always eat like it's our last meal," he said, "and since we're doing something extremely dangerous, let's make sure we enjoy it to the fullest."

He knew this would cost him a great deal, as the only currency accepted in this resort was the U.S. dollar, and the communist prices for tourists were outrageous. He ordered three jumbo shrimp cocktails, three steamed lobsters with white rice, black beans, ripe fried bananas, and for the greatest elegance, a bottle of fine imported wine from California, my own backyard for so many years. I looked at the bottle and saw that it was a BV Pinot Grigio. It wasn't a bad wine by any means and one I had frequently had. It also wasn't a particularly expensive wine, perhaps going for six or seven dollars in California. When they brought the check, I glanced at it and saw that they charged my uncle $180 for the bottle.

I shook my head and smiled. It was over 2,500% profit for the Cuban government. I started to laugh. It was ironic that early in the Revolution, the Cuban government had confiscated even the smallest businesses, accusing the owners of being thieves who bought a product for $10 and sold it for $15 or $20; in a capitalist society, that was a logical margin. It not only provided sufficient profit for the owner to live on, but it also allowed them to pay their employees enough to feed *their* families in turn. In the communist demagogy, the business owners were accused of being parasites who nourished themselves from the blood of the poor people they abused. This was how the government brainwashed the people into dismantling the free enterprise system that had existed in exchange for the false socialist promises of free products and services for all without any extra charges. The irony was that now the poor people were being severely rationed, and the Cuban government, based on that profit margin, were thieves without any competition at all.

My uncle noticed my laughter. With a smile on his face, he asked, "Is there something here on the table bringing memories of the past to you?"

"Yes, very much. You must be psychic." I picked up the bottle of wine. "Do you know how much this bottle costs in a California restaurant?"

Still smiling, he said, "Sure, probably seventy-five to a hundred dollars."

I shook my head and grinned. In spite of all the years he had lived under a socialist regime, he still had a capitalist mindset. I said, "You're a long way short in your pricing. In a restaurant, the most I've paid for a bottle like that is $20. I don't want to ruin your appetite, but you asked me for the truth." My uncle grabbed at his stomach and grimaced.

"That's not the worst, my uncle. In a market liquor store, when it's not on sale, the most I've paid for this bottle is $6."

My uncle lay his head down on the table and groaned. He came back up, holding his forehead with his left hand as he closed his eyes in discontent. "What else can you expect from these bandits?" He raised a hand. "Listen, *que sera sera*. It's only money. Let's finish the bottle. This is only one more reason to hate these bloodsuckers and continue to inflict the most damage we can to them."

We finished the bottle. "One hundred eighty dollars!" Tanya exclaimed. "You could buy a used car for that in the States."

A little later, we reviewed our plans. Tanya helped me attach the multiple cameras we were putting in my clothing. I had brought three different audio and video systems with me. We wanted to make certain that, after all our effort, that there was no risk of any malfunction in any of the electronics. We wanted to get every possible angle of every terrorist's face that was attending that conference. We especially wanted to capitalize on information about those who were supposed to participate in what bin Laden called "the most ambitious terrorist act in the history of humanity."

We carefully made small holes for the cameras all over my costume, even over my back, so that I could film people while I appeared to be looking in the exact opposite direction. My passport and ID papers were those of a Saudi Arabian multimillionaire business man of Greek origin by the name of Abdul Hasan Nassir. We had been following this man for a long time. He was a personal friend of bin Laden's, but he had also been his right arm in moving vast quantities of money from one country to another for use in secret operations. He had financed al-Qaeda and joined forces with the Tricontinental Union.

I had studied him intensively so that I could impersonate him exactly, and I had brought with me a letter signed by bin Laden given to Nassir, which read, *To Whom It May Concern, the bearer of this letter, Abdul Hasan Nassir, is a great friend of mine and a businessman with unimpeachable reputation in the service of the cause of jihad and Allah. He is one of my most trusted associates. He possesses the most intimate knowledge of our organization and has proven to us his value as a great leader and supervises our internationalist revolutionary plans. For that reason, I have assigned him as the leader of our movement al-Qaeda in the territorial zones of East Africa. Please facilitate him with whatever he needs and offer him all courtesies. He speaks with my authority, and in proof this document is signed in the City of Nairobi in the Country of Kenya, the 17th day of March, 1997.*

I had copies of this document translated in English, French, and Spanish as well. The original was in Arabic, with bin Laden's direct signature. In truth, the only forgery in this entire package was myself. As covers went, it was as perfect and airtight as possible, so long as Nassir himself never showed up. Since the conference was due to start in a few hours, we had little fear of that happening.

We went over and verified every detail and tested all the equipment. Tanya, however, was a little worried, and said, "Whatever happens, the only thing you cannot allow is to get caught with this equipment on you. Remember, if you have any doubts at all, stop—do not proceed. Get rid of everything and abort the mission, no matter how much it would break your heart. We will always have another opportunity; you only have one life."

I smiled at her in gratitude. I shook my head, "Another opportunity like this? I don't think so. But don't worry about it; I have no intention to meet many virgins in Paradise today like these lunatics. If I have no exit but to abort the plan, I will do it without hesitation, no matter how deeply it wounds my heart. I know what they're planning is nothing good and will cost the lives of hundreds if not thousands of innocent people. For their sake, I will give my best effort to destroy their plans."

My uncle finished putting on his bulletproof vest and offered me another. I refused it, however. I already had too much on me, and adding the vest might make me look overweight. Since Nassir was not, this might catch some unwanted attention.

My uncle said, "Listen, when one lives the life of the rich and famous, it's only natural for one to put on a few extra pounds. The worst they can do is tease you for being a little plump; better that, though, than to wind up dead."

My uncle's strong insistence meant that the vest went on my body. We finally left the bungalow at 6:00 p.m. in separate cars. Tanya and I left in the small MG convertible which had belonged to her niece Maggie. Tanya had kept it all these years for sentimental reasons. My uncle drove off in his light green and beige Plymouth Fury, headed towards Miramar.

The area was very secluded; before the Revolution, the rich and famous, including Cuban multimillionaires, had lived in these gated communities. This particular area had a small lake enclosed, and the addition was named El Laguito.

Cuban Mansion in El Laguito

We were getting close to the place. My uncle used his headlights to signal to us and then drove away to position himself to help cover our exit. We continued down the immense driveway lined on both sides with coconut trees. We approached the sentry booth which contained security guards armed to the teeth. They asked for identification, and I showed them my papers. The guard went inside and telephoned someone. After a few moments, he came back out, handed our papers back, and motioned us forward as he commanded the guard to lift the gate.

After we drove through, Tanya crossed herself and said, "Well, we've gotten past the first obstacle. You know what? No matter how many years I've been doing this, it always feels like the first time. I get this strange feeling that starts right beneath my ribs and shoots right back to my tailbone. It then shoots straight to my stomach. Does this happen to you, too, or is it just me?"

I smiled. "No. Remember, we're not all equal like the communists say. We're all different. I don't get the tickling in my stomach or a pain in my tailbone or anything like that, but I get sweaty hands." I took her hand with one of mine.

"Oh, what do you have there, a lagoon?" she exclaimed. "If you get nervous for too long, we might need to get some paddles out."

I took out a handkerchief and wiped my hand. We both smiled, and she continued to drive along the beautiful gardens of that resplendent estate. She continued, "I ask myself why romance doesn't function the same way. It might be extraordinary at first, but after a certain amount of time it becomes routine. I wish it were like fear and nervousness, which always produces the feathers in the stomach and the kick in the tailbone—or, in your case, sweaty palms. That way, the flame of passion always burns brightly like the pilot light in the water heater in your house."

We drove up to the main entrance of the mansion. Several valets came down to greet us. One asked Tanya if she wanted them to park the car or if she preferred to do it herself. She said she wanted to park, and they directed her where to go. She drove to where they had directed her and found a space. We got out and started to walk between the other cars.

Something caught my attention. It was a car that looked familiar to me. A beautiful woman with Asian features stepped out. Our eyes met and she smiled at me. I returned the smile, but otherwise didn't give much importance to the gesture. She was dressed in what appeared to be a nice, white uniform. She looked like she might be a nurse or a chef. It could also have been, I thought, culturally typical attire for whatever country she came from.

We continued to walk towards the house. Tanya had insisted on self-parking to make certain we retained full access to the car in case we had to leave suddenly. It would not have been smart if we needed to first have a valet fetch the car, especially if the cause for our departure was a violent one.

We saw many soldiers patrolling the perimeter of the building. We were stopped only briefly, as we had already penetrated the primary line of defense. We were directed to the door of the house, where agents for state security were doing a more careful check of documents before allowing entry to the mansion. The people lined up to enter were all dressed in civilian clothes.

When we reached the government agents, we had to first present the invitation to the conference before displaying the rest of our papers. The chief agent raised his eyebrows as he read my letter. They recorded our names and took our photographs. The agent gave me a big smile, and with extreme courtesy returned our papers. They printed and laminated badges with our names and photos, and these were attached to silk necklaces for us to wear. They informed us that different badges granted different access, and ours allowed us to go anywhere. They gave us directions to the first ballroom on the left, where an excellent buffet was set up. We thanked them and went inside, heading towards the buffet.

The ballroom was vast, filled with tables like a conference room. The food was varied: Asian, Cuban, African, Middle Eastern. The Cuban cuisine was fairly typical, featuring a roasted pig with an apple in its mouth and grapes imported from Canada. The table set up with Middle Eastern cuisine had a lamb, with its head still attached, roasted and garnished with mint and boiled eggs. I took some lamb and went to another table. I figured it must be for Middle Eastern guests, even though they were a minority of the people there.

We also took some assorted fruit and cheeses, even though we had no appetite. Between the splendid lunch and our tension, any desire for food had quite vanished. However, we needed to blend in, and it was Tanya who was going to seek out each individual on our list, looking for the name tags. She was dressed like a beautiful model and was sure to attract the attention of anyone there. Her task was to start conversations, and when I was needed she would signal me. I was looking for either an affectionate, flirtatious pat on the shoulder or a hand around his neck. I would then make sure one of my cameras caught that individual without getting close to anyone.

It was going to be time-consuming. We estimated there were between 285 and 300 men and women present. Apart from the Middle Eastern men, there were also people from Cuban, Venezuelan, and Central and South American, and African countries floating around. There were naturally a large number of G-2 agents circulating the crowd, as well as the possibility of other counter-intelligence personnel there. Our work started as we separated so that Tanya could mark the first target for me after she verified his name from his tag.

I moved forward and began to film him from as many angles as I could. For the next several hours we continued our work undetected. Occasionally we got back together for a few seconds to have a drink of champagne to maintain our cover. In between my chats with Tanya and the work we were doing taking pictures, I observed that the woman with Asian features was keeping her eyes on both of us. I was beginning to grow nervous, although she could have been looking at us out of curiosity because we were such an oddly-matched couple.

I pulled out the laundry list of terrorists that bin Laden had sent to Cuba for training and spiritual retreat before sending them on their huge mission in the U.S. Our informants had told us that this mission was scheduled to take place very soon. The deal between Castro and bin Laden was that Cuba would provide his guerillas lessons not just in piloting flight simulators but also logistics training and physical conditioning at Cuban Air Force bases. Every one of these jihadist terrorists, logically enough, was using a pseudonym. They had assumed names of actual Saudi Arabian pilots, stealing not only their identities but also their legal passports, complicit with the corrupt immigration officials who took a vast sum of money for their services.

This made certain that these men could not be stopped by any means. Their passports corresponded to legitimate individuals who customarily entered and left the United States. This is why it was imperative for us to place those names on my short list and match those names with the faces we found at the party, so that our people in the border crossings at Mexico and Canada would know who to look for as they entered the U.S. to execute bin Laden's masterpiece.

We finally finished our work to our total satisfaction. Tanya and I had taken photographs at every single angle, even from behind. We had also recorded every detail of the conference, revealing what the terrorists proposed to do. Nothing, however, was spoken openly. Our enemies were being extremely careful to not speak in details about what their plans where; all such conversation was couched in highly rhetorical terms, as if they were speaking in metaphors. We determined that our time there was coming to an end. Prolonging our stay would be to invite unnecessary risk at this point.

One of the al-Qaeda leaders spoke, telling the crowd, "Finally, the dream of our great warrior, Ernesto 'Ché' Guevara, will come true." I had to drink a little more champagne to keep from vomiting and wash that deception down. Tanya murmured, "I think we've gotten what we need. I think I need to go lock myself in the bathroom of my house. Speaking of which, I need to go for physiological needs."

I smiled. "I do, too, but it's not for any other reason than drinking too much champagne."

She nodded. "Me, too. OK, let's meet in the other salon by the exit doors."

"OK, let's go." She took my arm, and we started to walk towards the restrooms.

As we started that way, I could see two soldiers in full uniform. Up until this point, they were the only uniformed personnel inside—all the others had remained outside. They held their firearms at the ready, clearly searching for somebody. They walked in our direction, and my eyes met those of the chief, who had come in with them next to another man in civilian clothes— probably another state security agent.

My alert level increased. Tanya felt the same. "I have that tickling in my tailbone," she murmured as she squeezed my arm.

"Keep walking. Just increase your pace. We need to get to the bathroom quickly, after all."

What increased my concern was seeing the woman in white entering right behind them. She gestured vaguely in our direction. The chief held some sheaves of paper in his hand. He looked extremely angry, as if something was wrong. The corridor curved at the end, leading one to the bathrooms.

I said to Tanya, "You get into the ladies' room and don't worry about me, OK? I'll manage."

We picked up our pace without running. I heard the chief yell behind me, "Mr. Nassir! Please, stop—we have a question to ask you."

We ignored him and turned the corner at that moment. A man stood outside the ladies' bathroom. At that moment, a woman emerged, and the two of them walked past us. Tanya quickly let go of my arm. "What are you going to do?" "Don't worry. Follow the plan. I'll handle myself, and you handle yourself, just like we planned. Goodbye." Tanya jumped into the ladies' room. I shoved open the door to the men's room but ran further down the corridor to the next door. Fortunately, when I pushed on it, it was unlocked, and I ducked inside to find myself in a utility room. I looked around for an exit, but there were iron bars outside the windows, which were too high up to reach regardless. I kept going and found a narrow corridor. I went down it and found myself in the kitchen, still looking for an exit.

I heard a noise behind me as the door opened. I ducked under one of the work tables which held several pots and pans. It didn't look terribly safe to me, so I moved to the underside of another table, this one laden with Asian food—perhaps used as a reloading station for the buffet. I looked for an even safer space. Looking to my right, I found a space cluttered with utensils and squeezed in.

I heard steps of people entering the kitchen, and the lights came fully on. A man and woman, attired similarly to the other woman I had been seeing—but with the addition of chef's hats—carried empty platters which they went over to refill, circulating to other tables I had not noticed before.

I carefully watched every single step they made. They were immediately before the place I was concealed, but the clutter hid me from their view. They stopped what they were doing and turned in my direction abruptly, freezing in their tracks. It felt as if they had seen me. They started to slowly raise their hands over their heads.

I turned my head to see what was going on. On the other side of the shelves, I heard a man's voice say authoritatively, "Don't even move, or you will not live to tell of your adventure as an imposter." At that, I slowly raised my arms. Out of the corner of my eye I could see the chief pointing his pistol at me. A corpulent guard was next to him with a submachine gun trained on me. "Get out of there," he said insistently. "You will probably go from here to the firing squad."

All of the service personnel remained frozen with their hands up. I slowly got out of my hiding place, wondering how I was going to get out of this one.

He smiled sarcastically and asked, "Who are you working for?" Without waiting for an answer, he went on, "Certainly for the CIA or British intelligence."

I shook my head immediately and replied, "You are in very great error. I know you're looking for somebody, but it's not me."

He yelled, "Do you think we are stupid because we're a Third World country and you come from Gringolandia? We know who you are. We've already checked your fingerprints that you left on your papers. Just come out of there now, or I will kill you here now without blinking an eye. I'll get the highest medal from the Revolution, considering who you are."

"OK, OK," I replied, "I'm coming out."

I was just getting out from the shelves. He took a step forward, and a loud metallic clang resounded as a cast iron skillet impacted the skull of the guard. He collapsed heavily onto the floor, his machine gun still held to his chest. The chief turned to see what had happened. I snatched one of the knives I had been eyeing as I left the hiding place. With all my strength, I hurled it at him. He was only a few steps away, and so the momentum of the throw sent the knife almost entirely through his neck. However, it did not hit his spine or either of the great blood vessels in his neck. He fired his pistol twice, hitting me both times in the chest.

The impact flung me back onto one of the tables of food. I slid across the table, spilling food all over the floor. As I flew back, I saw an enormous frying pan swing through the air, smashing into the chief's head with such force that he fell to his knees, the knife still sticking out of his throat. He then crumpled onto the floor.

A few seconds later, the attractive woman with Asian features stepped out. She ran to my side after checking that both men were knocked out. She asked, "Are you OK? I'm Yein Xiang, Chandee's sister. You remember me?"

I nodded, still a little dazed. "Your uncle asked me to guard you," she said. "I'm sorry I failed you; I was a little late."

I smiled and opened my shirt to reveal the vest. "Oh, thank God!" she exclaimed with a large smile on her face. She yelled to the service people in Mandarin, rapping out orders.

As if propelled by springs, they were all shaken out of their lethargy and moved into action, hastily obeying her orders. They put the bodies of the two men into laundry baskets they had brought in, after hitting each of them with a pot. I wasn't sure if they didn't want them to return to consciousness or if it was out of retaliation for previous ill treatment. Fast as lightning they brought a thermal cart for food, and Yein said, "Get into this cart. We'll get you out of here, safe and sound."

I smiled. Before I got into the cart, I shook my head and said, "To think I've been worrying all night that you might be working with them."

She gave me a quick kiss on my cheek. "For the communists, the people who murdered my father? Never!"

With no doubts left in my mind, I knew I was in good hands, and so I entrusted myself to her and her people. Inside the cart, I felt as if I were being rolled all over the place by her employees. I heard Yein giving orders as she followed them. After we left the kitchen, I heard a gentle rap on the door of the cart.

"Don't worry about it if you hear any explosions, OK?" she said. "Stay in there at all costs. I put some heavy explosives in some cars in the parking lot as a decoy in case we needed to get out of here like this. That will keep everyone distracted for a while."

I was able to see through the crack at the top of the door. I heard a click like a remote control being activated, and six explosions erupted in a chain around the area. She said very softly, "The power of ITN explosives."

Through the crack in the cart, I could see the lines of smoke. I saw people running all over the place as they tried to leave in panic. They loaded me into a van. I could see on one of the doors a sign which read, *International Gourmet Food: Specialists in Cuban, Asian Exclusive Service to Embassies, Resorts, and Hotels.*

We reached the exit gate, and there was another click from the remote control. A beeping sound was heard, and six more explosions went off. The carts inside the van, including mine, rocked back and forth violently. I thought to myself that this pretty Chinese girl had become a pyromaniac. I could hear the laughter of Yein and her associates as they celebrated their actions. I heard the pop of a champagne cork.

A few minutes later, I could hear the horn of the van honk out the old "shave and a haircut" rhythm, which was repeated by another horn outside—I recognized the sound of my uncle's car horn. The van stopped, and I heard the sound of the door opening. Then the thermal cart was opened up, and I saw my uncle extending his hand to help me up.

A thousand smells from the assorted food assailed my nostrils. I held a small, silver container in my hand with fried wontons, eating one with my fingers as I emerged. Apparently it had been forgotten in all the excitement. I said, "How lucky you left me something to eat. I've been snacking all this time." I offered them to everyone as we laughed.

"Are you all right?" my uncle asked.

"Yes, I'm fine, thanks be to God. And let's not forget Yein." I opened my shirt and lifted the vest to show the brilliant purpling bruise left from the two shots intercepted by the vest. My uncle crossed himself.

"You're right. Thank God that I had to practically twist your arm to wear that vest. If you didn't have that on, today would not have finished the way it did, and I would have lived the rest of my life with that remorse on my conscience for not pushing you hard enough to wear it."

Yein inserted herself into the conversation. "OK, OK. We have to move quickly. Just remember that I still have to go to the government department where I work to drop the empty carts and pick up the rest. Follow what we agreed on: drop him at my house and I will take care of him from there and get him to the airport after I get back from the job."

She turned to me. "I'll get my car and meet you at my house. We have to go back to the party and clean up or my people will be exposed." She handed me an airplane ticket for Mexico. "All you have to do is change into a different disguise and wait patiently for me. You know which disguise to take."

I smiled and gave her a kiss on the cheek. "OK. Thank you again. I owe you my life."

"No, don't thank me," she said. "Thank your uncle. I almost failed you. There is a good reason our parents told us to listen to our elders."

We both smiled. After we said goodbye, I got into my uncle's car. We drove off towards Chinatown in Old Havana. As we drove to Yein's house, I remembered how many times on previous occasions I had used this particular route through town in order to pick up Yein's sister Chandee from her house. Chandee had been a great help to me in my clandestine work when I was still living in Cuba.

Havana's Old Chinatown

My uncle broke into my thoughts when he handed me a small mini-cassette recorder with audio phones. He said, "This is the result of the great work of freedom fighters infiltrating inside the G-2. This particular tape cost the life of one of them. It's something that has just happened in the last few hours. It's as important as the information you came into this country today to acquire and bring back to our sources. Thank God you got that done, but maybe this information is equally or even more important. It can destabilize the whole region, including Central and South America."

He gestured to his ears to mimic using the earphone. "Listen to the tape."

I could see how anxious he was for me to hear the information, so I put the wires in my ear. He said, "Press the red button that reads 'play.'"

I didn't want to disrespect him. I knew that already, so I just nodded my head, smiled, and pressed the play button.

I heard Benny More music and looked at him incredulously. He circled his hand in the air to indicate that I should keep listening. "Yeah, music is there as a decoy. The information comes in after the music." As he said that, the music stopped, and I heard a conversation. I was thrown by the implications of what I heard. I rubbed my forehead in distress.

After listening to the tape all the way through, I switched it off and rolled the wires around it. "Oh, my God—even after listening to that with my own ears, it is difficult to comprehend the level of sadism these people will stoop to in order to accomplish their goals. That's not even considering what they're willing to do to take the lives of an entire family, women and children included." I shook my head in disbelief as I handed the recorder back to him with my left hand.

He shook his head. "No, no—that's for you. This is now a separate mission that you should give high priority. You need to do whatever you can to prevent this from taking place. Don't stop at any method you think you may have to use in the process. Whatever happens, though, remember that nobody can have a copy of it and can only listen to it under your direct supervision. You can show it to the people you need to hear it. That tape includes voices not just of our enemies but also voices of our friends. They have already put their lives at risk to take that information out of the highest levels of the government in an attempt to stop this operation."

I nodded. I put the mini-recorder in one of my bags. "You don't have to worry about a thing. I will do it exactly the way you ask. After the important people who need to hear it have listened and I get the response I need to proceed with a plan in order to stop it, I will destroy the tape. Believe me, I know the consequences of this landing in the hands of our enemies, the damage it could bring to those freedom fighters we have implanted inside Castro's circle."

My uncle put his right hand on my shoulder and gave me a slight squeeze. "A woman is not just involved in this crime they're planning. She is the main contact and one of the principle executors of the plan. If you have any trouble with your conscience in putting these guys out of commission because of that, just think about for a minute what they're intending to do, and I assure you that you will find peace with yourself."

He took a manila envelope out of his sport coat and handed it to me. "Right here you will see the pictures of each of the people contracted to perform this operation."

We arrived at Yein's house. As always, we went to the alley behind the complex of buildings and went up the driveway there. My uncle got out of the car and handed me the key to the house. I picked up my handbag from the back seat and we hugged. "Good luck," he said, "and God bless you and help you get out of the country safely."

"Thank you, Uncle," I replied. "Good luck to you. God bless you as well."

In my left hand I took the envelope he had just given me, and my right held my bag. I closed the large wooden door on the patio after my uncle drove off and then entered by the concealed door. Given the late hour of the night, all the businesses were closed inside the complex, and I walked through the empty corridor until I got to the secret door that led to the dining room of Yein's house.

Not Quite the Same Coin

People who normally are arrogant and insecure, when they do a favor for you or anyone else, love to drag their feet to mortify you, make you beg, all the while making it sound like they are giving you their life's blood in doing it. It gets to the point that you no longer want that favor any more, even though you intend without revealing to them that you plan to return that favor multiplied many times over in the future. It doesn't matter how grateful you can be, they will unnecessarily brag about the fact to mark their superiority because of what you need at that moment from them.

Your intellect tells you to be rid of such people, but in your goodness you swallow your humiliation, simply because you need that thing done. You also want to be mature enough to accomplish the goal and you unnecessarily endure patiently the long, unpleasant moments those people force you to experience. I never forget the goodness and the ugliness in people, gratefully and pleasantly retaining in my mind the thought when the time comes I will make these people wait for a very long tomorrow with a very large smile on my face, a red rose without any thorns in my hand, and forgive them for my previous humiliations. Still smiling broadly, I will take my sweet time and give them the same sad flavor in their throats that they gave to me. Their past mercenary actions will indeed be repaid, but not in quite the same coin.

Dr. Julio Antonio del Mármol

Chapter 3

A DANGEROUS WAY OUT

After I entered, I looked around nostalgically. Everything there looked the same as the last time I had visited so many years ago. Like Cuba, nothing had changed in all those decades save for increased deterioration and overall bad condition. I walked into what had once been Chandee's room. Memories flooded my brain as I remembered the beautiful, romantic moments with her, listening to the rock music of Paul Anka, how we made love for the first time along the riverbank near Rio Cristal. I let myself drop onto the bed and looked up at the ceiling. I remained there for a while, letting my mind float along those lovely memories that now seemed strangely close and recent.

Some time had passed, and the small cuckoo clock on the wall began to chirp the hour. I started up, because there was still much to do before I left the country and nowhere near enough time to spend in reverie.

I rolled out of bed and looked through my travel bag. I pulled out the things I needed to change into my new disguise. I removed the clothing and the prosthetic nose. I took all the wires, cameras, and microphones out of my clothes and hid them inside a secret compartment in the travel bag, cunningly built into a double bottom that one wouldn't even feel during a search. I put everything I was going to bring back to O'Brien, my contact in the U.S. government, into an envelope. I left out the mini-cassette player my uncle had given me. I decided the best way to hide something was to leave it in plain view, and I left it mixed in with my electric razor, colognes, and other items that would, I assumed, not even be noticed by the customs agents at the airport.

I hopped into the shower and quickly washed off the aroma accumulated from the food residue inside the cart. I then proceeded to straighten my hair using the chemicals I had brought with me for that purpose. Using some bleach, I changed my hair color to pure white. I trimmed my beard very short and dyed it white as well. I tried to appear much older than I was. As an elderly man, our enemies in the customs service would look at me as someone who wouldn't attempt something crazy. I put on a Panama hat with a bandana that matched my shirt. I looked at myself in the mirror over the bathroom sink and checked my passport. I needed to adjust my nose to match the photo—it needed to be thinner and turned up at the end.

I went through my bag of prosthetic noses and found a good match. I applied some adhesive to the prosthetic and placed it on my nose, maintaining pressure with my fingers until it was firmly attached. I checked the photo on my Mexican passport again, and my reflection matched exactly. I smiled in satisfaction and picked up my umbrella. I tested the weapons systems in the umbrella and made sure it was loaded. I picked up my crocodile skin portfolio and looked myself over in the mirror once more after donning my sunglasses. I nodded in approval, removed my sunglasses, and put them in the front pocket of my suit.

I put the gold Tag Heuer watch with a sky blue face on my left arm, and the multifunction silver chronometer scuba watch on my right. I pulled two rings—one of which was a deadly weapon— out of a small box. I checked to make sure it was functional and slipped it on my right hand. The other, a sapphire ring with the emblem of our freedom fighter group, I slipped onto my left.

I packed everything else into my travel bag with the exception of my previous disguise. Everything related to that identity I put on the bed. I went into the kitchen to locate a metal trash can. I emptied the small amount of refuse into a corner of the kitchen and took the container into the bedroom. I dropped everything from my previous identity into it and sprinkled cologne all over it. I lit the contents on fire and for safety's sake brought the can into the kitchen. I watched it burn and waited until the flames died down enough that no chance of an accident remained. I left the burning disguise and went back into the bedroom to bring everything out into the kitchen.

While I did this, I heard some steps near the secret door. I immediately took precautions, snatching up my umbrella. I heard Yein's voice call out, "Julio Antonio, it's me. Don't shoot me, please." I smiled and left the room with the umbrella in my hand. She knew how dangerous it was and joked, "Please don't point that thing at me." She looked me up and down and said admiringly, "Ooh, la-la. That is the Julio Antonio I have in my memories, the one I had a crush on when I was a teenager."

I smiled. "That is very typical when we are very young. We have a tendency to get crushes on those who are more adult."

She smiled maliciously as I deposited my things by the table in the dining room. She looked at the small pile of trash in the corner and the still burning contents of the metal basket. She shook her head and said, "I know you are very famous in all of Cuba. Probably, after all these years, even all over the world, for creating gigantic commotions to distract your enemies wherever you go, leaving your signature lightning in the sky. But please don't destroy my house before you leave Cuba. It's the only thing I have left of my family."

I shook my head and could not hold back a laugh. I nudged the metal basket with my foot. "This is the only thing I could find in which I could safely burn my old disguise and documents, sweetie."

She held her hands up and shook her head. "I'm only joking, for God's sake." She spread her hands around to point out her father's old antique store and the very few items that remained. Many of the empty shelves were filled with cobwebs. She said sadly, "We have to thank the Revolution for this destruction. That is the true word for revolution: destruction. All they do is destroy all the work others have done. And for what? Only to satisfy the thirst for power of some politician and to make filthy rich a small group of ambitious individuals."

I thought for a few seconds about what she had said. She'd hit the nail right on the head. The real motive of many of the men who fought in that revolution wasn't to free anyone from Batista's regime; it was power. Later, without any regard for the consequences of their ambition, they destroyed the country.

Yein said, "We have almost two hours until you have to be at the airport. Why don't you sit down like in the old days when you would visit us, and share with me a cup of tea before you leave?"

I looked at her and she smiled insistently. She took my hand. "Come on, come on." I smiled and nodded in acceptance as I sat down next to her at the table.

She put the teapot on the fire. I asked, "Do you know if Tanya got out OK from the conference?"

She nodded emphatically. "Yes, yes—I'm sorry, I forgot to tell you. She left in her MG without any trouble. I saw her with my own eyes when I went to get my car. By the way, they held me back with a million questions before they let me leave. That's why I'm so late. Once they determined I hadn't had anything to do with what had happened there, they decided to let me go."

I breathed deeply in relief at the knowledge that Tanya was all right. I knew very well that she had been in the spy business for so long and had so much experience as an international operative that she must have had a very good alibi prepared should they question her.

Yein brought the cups of tea to the table. She brought the teapot over and filled two cups. She sat down next to me and gave me a very loving look, and for a moment I saw Chandee sitting there. The family resemblance was very strong. She was very pretty and rather sexy.

She said, "Wait a moment, I have a present for you." She darted out of the kitchen and returned a few moments later with a box in her hand. She handed it to me. I opened it and saw several sheets of paper, some photos, and a spool of old tape. I sorted through them and saw that one was my birth certificate from the municipal office in Guane. The blue seal was plainly there in one corner. My doctoral diploma from the University of Havana was also inside, though it appeared to have sustained water damage, along with some sheets of music. I looked at her in surprise. "How did you get this?"

Dr. del Mármol's Birth Certificate   **University Degree**

She took a little sip from her cup. "Your Mima. I visited her frequently until she was able to leave. I'm sorry some of those were damaged, but your house was hit by a hurricane a while back." She held up the spool of tape. "I've played this occasionally— it's an old recording session with your band, Las Gatos Negros. I think it was from about the same time those photos were taken. We also had to save your birth certificate. When you left Cuba, the government wanted to destroy your reputation and everything you accomplished. They erased all your records in the country: your elementary school, your records from the National School of

Arts, even from the university. You became a real ghost. You don't officially exist in this country."

Dr. del Mármol's Teen Band, Los Gatos Negros

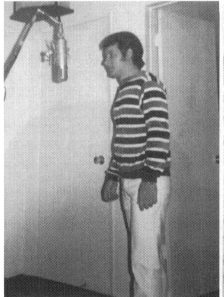

Recording Session   *"En Tu Cumpleaños"*

I shook my head. "What an irony. When I entered the United States, I became a ghost there, too."

"When we realized what they were doing and had already accomplished, my father sent me to Guane with your uncle and sister Disa. Luckily, we arrived there a few hours before they destroyed even your birth certificate. I've been saving it for you to place in your hands one day. Please don't tell your uncle I gave it to you, no matter what. They only reason they told me to save it was for when the government collapsed so that you could prove that you are a citizen here. But don't bring it with you on one of your trips, ever." She raised her eyebrows. "Can you imagine what the communists would do to you if they caught you with this document?"

I smiled easily. "No more than if they found me with what I'm transporting in my bag through that airport today."

I nudged the bag at my feet. I took her hand and kissed it. I looked into her eyes and said, "Thank you once more for that beautiful present which proves I was born here in my beautiful Cuba and discredits the intention of these miserable liars."

Yein looked at me sympathetically. "I knew you would like it."

She checked her watch. "Well, I think it's time to go. I think it will be better to be there ahead of time in case they decide to give you any problems in the airport."

I stood up and she gave me a hug. "I'm not going to walk with you to the airport," she said. "I'll leave you at the door. Those are the instructions I have from your uncle—you know him; I have to follow them. But I won't leave until I see your plane take off, in case you have any emergencies crop up. I'll be your getaway driver in that case."

I smiled. "I hope that won't be the case."

We left the house and drove to the airport. In the parking lot, I got my stuff out of the car, and she gave me one more hug and a friendly kiss on the lips. "God protect you," she said. "Take care of yourself."

"Thank you." I walked towards the entrance of the small airport. I entered the small room, a place I had not been in for nearly four decades. I was depressed in my spirit. After I had walked all over the world and seen so many beautiful airports, even in the poorest of countries, I saw the deplorable condition of that building. I had been to Cuba so many times, but my entry and exit had been by sea. The last time I had used the airport was when I had said goodbye to my big brother as he left Cuba for Spain.

Emigration Station, José Martí International Airport

I sat down on the corner of a rustic, uncomfortable seat. I kept my eyes on one of the customs agents, a man of medium height. He had bronzed skin, and was obviously a mix of several races, not taking on any good genes from any of the races within him.

He passed by me several times, looking at me. I tried to avoid his indiscrete looks, but a couple of times our eyes met. On those occasions, I gave him a courteous smile and a nod of greeting. I started to worry after a few minutes, thinking it might have been a big mistake to take Yein's suggestion of coming here early. It looked like I was catching too much attention. I knew that anyone working in customs who was also Cuban intelligence could create problems for me, especially given the cargo I was carrying. From a spy's point of view, I was transporting a nuclear warhead in that travel bag. If I were caught, it was certain I wasn't going to end up at Club Med.

The other passengers who were supposed to get on that flight began to arrive, and more people joined me in waiting. I started to feel more at ease. People started to line up for the gate. For the final time, the customs agent approached me and asked, "Do you have anything to declare?"

I shook my head and said in a firm, cordial voice, "No sir. Thank you for asking."

"In that case," he replied, "you don't have to be in line. Come on, follow me." He gestured to me.

For obvious reasons, this bothered me. He hadn't asked anyone else. I hadn't even gotten in line yet. Several agents were checking the passports and luggage of the rest of the passengers at a small table. I had no alternative but to do as he said and follow him.

He took me away from the door where others were being checked in, past fifty feet of glass partitions. People started to walk down the stairs onto the tarmac to board the plane. He sat down at a small table which looked more like a coffee table and pulled up a small chair. The *mestizo*[8] asked for my passport. He opened it with a dogged expression. Very gravely, he said, "Doctor, huh?"

Maintaining all my courtesy and decency, I said politely, "Yes, sir, Mr. Agent."

He raised his eyes to look at me. "A doctor in what?"

"PhD in animal genetics," I said, carefully controlling my irritation. However, my smile had left my face.

With even greater abruptness, he gestured as he said, "Give me your bag. What are you carrying in that portfolio?"

I gave him a dirty look this time. "Medical reports. Protein and fat analysis from the milk and cheese that *maybe* we intend to buy from your government."

His whole head raised up and he gave me an arrogant look. "From what part of Mexico?"

I replied with a little irony, "From Baja California, sir."

He smiled knowingly and shook his head. "I knew you had to be from the side very close to the gringos. You look like one of them. You don't have the stereotype of the Aztec people. Even your Spanish accent isn't Mexican."

That last raised the hairs on my neck. Clearly, he was going to give me some trouble. Behind him, I could also see two jeeps filled

---

[8]   Person of mixed European and Amerindian descent

45

with soldiers, each heading to cover a different entrance. Perhaps he had already summoned the authorities and was distracting me. I picked up my cigarette lighter and case and offered him a cigarette. He hesitated but then snatched a handful of cigarettes out of my holder and put them in his shirt pocket. He smirked knowingly as he observed, "North American cigarettes, eh?" Then he picked the tape recorder out of my bag.

"What is this? You said you don't have anything to declare, but this is electronic equipment." He pointed to the wall. "Don't you know how to read? There it is, in Spanish, English, and French. Can you read, Dr. Valentine?" He tapped the sign. "It says very clearly that every bit of electronic equipment will be confiscated by the Customs Agency and you will be subjected to a fine."

I smiled and breathed deeply before swallowing. "I'm sorry. I brought this with me from Mexico to record my notes, and it has some Cuban music I wanted to bring back. The truth is I didn't realize this small tape recorder would be considered 'electronic equipment.' It's battery powered."

At that moment, he pushed the play button, and the beautiful song from Benny More, "Santa Isabel de las Lajas," began to play. He smiled as he listened to the music. I prayed that he wouldn't listen much longer, since the song was a short one.

Two of the voices on that tape were those of none other than the communist politicians Ramiro Valdés and Raúl Castro.

My hands started to sweat. We were in the middle of a room with glass dividers everywhere save for the wall on the left. Beyond that were the offices for the airport's senior staff. In an act of desperation, I stood up and removed from my pants pocket a gold money clip with a couple thousand dollars. I peeled off a few bills, saying, "I'm very open to paying the penalty for disobeying the rules. Whatever you ask. But please—I don't want to leave behind my recorder with my music and my work notes. They are very important to me."

"Put that away," he said quickly, "put that away. Not here in the middle of the room in front of everyone's eyes." He looked at my clip covetously.

I opened my arms in a pleading gesture. "Please, whatever you ask me for, but please don't confiscate my work and my music."

The *mestizo* turned off the recorder right at the moment the music ended and a spoken voice began. I started to sweat bullets. He watched me replace the bills and clip back into my pocket.

"Well, well—whatever I ask for?" He stood up with my passport in his left hand and the tape recorder in his right.

He whispered to me, "Follow me. Maybe we can work this out. But never, never put money in front of others here in Cuba. There are a lot of jealous people here, and everybody has to do whatever is necessary to survive. In order to take my job, they can accuse you of bribing me and accuse me of accepting it. Then we'll both end up in a lot of trouble. You think this is a problem now? You don't want to see what will happen when you attempt to bribe an officer of the law."

I walked behind him into a small storage room with chairs stacked next to a couple of filing cabinets. I knew at once that he was going to try to rob me. He closed the door and switched on the lights.

"OK, where is the money clip you showed me before?" he asked.

I asked, "How much?"

When I pulled the clip out of my pocket, he snatched it out of my hand. He put it in his pocket before I could do anything. Then he handed me my passport and said, "OK, you can leave. Your plane will leave shortly. Use the door on the left. If anyone asks you, tell them that Ramiro Salgado already checked you out and authorized you to leave."

"But what about the recorder? We had a deal."

He dismissed me with a hand. "Go, go. I need it for my work."

The blood raced to my face and ears, but I held myself down. "This is not what we agreed."

"We didn't agree to anything."

"You have almost two thousand dollars and my gold clip. Now give me my tape recorder, please."

"I told you, get out of here, or I will accuse you of smuggling drugs in your luggage." He pulled a small bag of cocaine out of his pants. "I'll say I found this in your bags, and you'll never see the light of day again. Now get out of here before I change my mind. Fucking Mexican gringo *de mierda*⁹!"

I took my gold watch off and showed it to him. His eyes shone with more greed. He reached out for it. "Give me my tape recorder," I said to him, "and you can keep the watch. It's worth $38,000."

He snatched the watch. "Still, I'm keeping your recorder. Now get the fuck out of here."

As he looked at the watch, I activated the spring of the poison needle in my ring out and stabbed his hand. "Ouch! What did you do?" He moved forward with the intention of striking me, but I ducked back and jabbed him in the neck. His eyes turned glassy and he fell to his knees. He stared up at me as I took the recorder, watch, and money clip out of his pockets. I put them away and leaned him back a little. I looked right into his eyes. I could see some foam at the corner of his mouth and he began to convulse weakly.

"Look at me," I said. "You've got at most three minutes to live, and you're going to die in very horrible pain. But there's enough time for you to ask forgiveness of the Lord Jesus Christ for the abuses and extortions and other bad things you've been doing to the Cuban people and Heaven knows how many tourists. Maybe I just exacted some justice, because you might be the one who stole the wedding rings that belonged to my mother and father before they left the country not too long ago. These are the minutes before you face Final Judgement. May God have mercy on your soul."

I turned around to leave him, but my conscience checked me. I never really had become hardened to taking another person's life, and even then could only do it when my life was actively being threatened. This man had no idea who I actually was; he was just

---

⁹ Piece of shit

trying to line his pockets. He had no malicious intent to jeopardize my life.

Since time was critically of the essence right now, I quickly picked up my cigarette case. I opened a secret compartment in the back of it and pulled out an antidote vial. I rapidly administered two doses to him to counter the two doses of poison he had been given from my ring. Snapping the case shut, I picked up my travel bag and portfolio. After making certain the door was completely locked, I closed it.

I walked down the stairs onto the tarmac. I shook my head in disgust as I thought about the situation, but he had pushed me into a corner. I shook my briefcase in suppressed anger. Even though it would take him quite some time to recover, he certainly would realize I had been no ordinary tourist. As soon as he was able to, he would report that to the authorities, who would then know which flight I had been on and would alert their contacts in Mexico City. Something or someone would likely be waiting for me there. I had to be alert and on my guard. I much preferred this, though, to having an unnecessary death on my conscience.

José Martí International Airport Tarmac

I walked hurriedly over the tarmac to join the line of people waiting to board the plane. I never had to use his name, as I arrived there unchallenged. I boarded the *Cubana de Aviación* flight. Shortly after, the airplane took off, and I looked back to see the island of Cuba, as I had a few decades before, disappear beneath my feet into the same uncertainty the near future would bring to me.

I asked the Lord to give me the strength to complete successfully my plans. I had to save the lives of so many innocent people who had not the slightest idea the danger they faced. I had seen with my own eyes the created beast—the war between good and evil, like in the past holy wars, which every one of us has the moral duty to avoid. I also asked Him to give me the power I needed to repel all the evil forces that were spreading like a cancer all across the world. I promised myself even if I had to spill the last drop of my blood, I would strive my best to stop it.

After a few glasses of champagne, which was the only thing one could purchase on that airline, I fell sound asleep. Three hours later, the plane landed in Mexico City, the Aztec capital. I woke with a smile on my face. I repeated my thanks to God for being back once more in the free world and for helping me escape alive from the claws of the evil government of the island of Cuba. There, in secret silence, they planned the conquest of the world through the terrorist network they had developed through the Tricontinental Union.

Chapter 4

THE IMPROVISED MISSION

Mexico City
December 21, 2000
12:00 a.m.

My *Cubana de Aviación* flight had just landed in Mexico. I was wearing a white suit and a Panama hat, carrying an umbrella, and holding a crocodile skin portfolio in my right hand. I looked like a millionaire playboy. Perhaps my attire was the reason Ramiro Salgado had singled me out back in Cuba.

As I walked through the airport terminal towards the baggage claim area, I saw an old blind man wearing dark sunglasses and holding a cup for donations. He quickly tucked something under his clothes as I approached. It looked like it might have been the kind of cell phone we used in intelligence, and my suspicions rose. I paused by him and dropped a handful of coins in his cup to get a better look at him and continued on my way. My suspicions grew as it appeared his skin wasn't as weathered as one would expect on a man of his apparent age. I knew now that I had to keep my eyes open. Now that I thought about it, I remembered I had seen that same man sitting in the back of the plane.

I retrieved my luggage and headed towards the terminal exit to call for a taxi. The next in line moved forward and stopped in front of me. Two men were seated in the back seat, but the black tinted windows of the cab concealed them from casual view. One of them exited by the left side, while the other rolled down his window and smiled at me.

The man who had gotten out pulled out a pistol with a silencer attached. He aimed it at me using the roof of the cab for stability and fired. I moved the portfolio to shield my head, just in time for the bullet to ricochet off, sparks flying from the case. I trained my umbrella up and the distinctive pop of a silenced gunshot sounded. The man collapsed, a hole oozing blood from his forehead. The other man pulled his own gun to shoot at me.

Bulletproof Briefcase

I swung my umbrella and slapped the gun out of his hand. It rolled into the gutter. I pressed the tip of the umbrella against him and demanded, "Who sent you?"

The man stared at me in terror. I repeated my question. "Who sent you, damn it?" I moved the tip to press against his throat. His eyes bulged in terror. "You have only a couple of seconds to tell me before I send you to Hell."

In his desperation, the man made a move, reaching for what looked like a gun or another weapon. I pressed a button on the umbrella, and a spring-loaded twelve-inch blade snapped out and into his neck, piercing his Adam's apple. The driver reached under the blanket next to his seat and pulled a revolver.

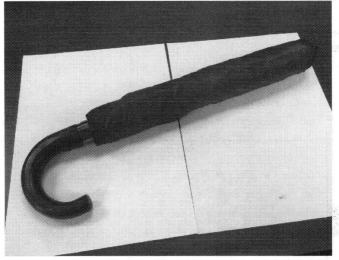

Umbrella Weapon

He aimed it at me and yelled, "What are you doing?" He fired twice.

I once again used the portfolio as a shield, and more sparks shot out as the bullets bounced off. The driver stomped on the accelerator and peeled out of there, the tires squealing in protest, leaving the one dead body behind, taking the other in the back seat with him. A crowd had started to gather, and there were screams.

Two police officers, attracted by the commotion, rushed in my direction. One of them yelled at me, "Stop! Stop!"

I started to run into the crowd. The police officer fired two warning shots into the air. Two police cars pulled up in an attempt to block my flight. In the confusion, I managed to get inside the terminal. I walked directly towards a door marked "Employees Only" in both English and Spanish.

I closed the door behind me and walked down the darkened corridor. I pulled a large key chain out from my coat pocket and flipped through the keys. I reached a metal security door marked "Authorized Access Only." Behind me, I could hear screams from the panicked crowd.

A voice yelled, "He ran through that door!"

I was perspiring heavily, not just from the exertion of running, but also from the heat of the corridor. I looked at two keys and tried the first one. It didn't work. I tried the second one, and the door opened. As I went through, the outer door also opened, and I heard the pounding of footsteps behind me.

I snatched my portfolio and umbrella and slipped inside, slamming the heavy security door shut behind me. The police officers tried the latch, and I heard one say, "Do you have the key to this door?"

"No," the other said, "only supervisors have the keys. This is a top security area. We're not even supposed to be in there."

The first officer appeared to be the senior. He pulled out a radio and said into it, "We need someone with access to the generator room."

More officers arrived outside, including a sergeant. "Go around!" he commanded. "Cover all the exits. We have a dead man on the ground. We have to find this guy."

I leaned against the other side of the door, getting my bearings. I listened to their conversation as my eyes tried to penetrate the pitch-black darkness of the room. I felt around and finally found the light switch. Flipping it on, I found myself in a large room filled with generators, electrical panels, and monitors with computers. Outside a window, I could see the traffic. I saw the entrance to a large restroom and went inside.

I took my clothes off and turned my jacket inside out, revealing the black inner material. I did the same with my pants, shirt, and belt. The hat was also adjustable. I transformed it into a baseball cap with a long visor, inverting the material to the black facing. The end result looked like the kind of cap worn by the FBI or Mexican Federales.

I pulled two bottles and a basin out of my briefcase. I mixed the contents of the bottles into the basin. I applied the dark color into my hair and beard, rapidly but efficiently. I rinsed the brush and began to use it to color my shoes from white to black. I wiped my shoes down with paper towels.

I checked my watch and saw that fifteen minutes had passed. I opened a chamber in the umbrella which looked much like that of a pistol. I loaded two rounds into the chamber and pushed the button on the umbrella to spring the blade. Carefully, I washed the blood off of the blade in the sink and then tested the blade to ensure it was still working properly.

I reached into my briefcase and switched my Versace sunglasses for larger sunglasses with a lighter tint. I checked the borders to make sure the crystals that allowed for rearview vision were in good order. I checked myself in the mirror and then turned to look myself over. A piece of fabric on the back of one pant leg was turned out in the back, revealing white. I fixed it and then opened the back door a crack to make sure I was still alone.

I pulled out my passport and slipped it into my coat pocket. I saw a door that led to the outside. I went over and opened it slightly. Through the crack I could see a taxi that was leaving the underground garage after dropping off a fare. I slipped out, and ran in front of the cab.

The driver looked up at me and said, "*A donde va, mi amigo*[10]?"

"*Al Centro*[11]," I said.

"OK," he replied, "*subase*[12]."

---

[10] Where are you going, my friend?
[11] Downtown
[12] Get in

I climbed inside the taxi, and he pulled away. However, we both could see the police putting roadblocks ahead of us. They were checking every car and ours was next.

The driver said, "There was a bad shooting at the airport. Probably narcotics trafficking. They told me there were ten deaths, five policemen and five bystanders."

I shook my head in amusement. "Oh, my God," I said. "I don't know where these drugs will end. This is unbelievable! Right in the middle of the airport."

The driver moved forward and the policeman approached him. "Where are you guys going?" he asked.

"Downtown," the driver replied.

The police officer looked into the back of the car and scrutinized me. I handed him my passport. I said, "We are going downtown, sir."

He looked at the passport. He read aloud, "Dr. Ricardo Barriety Valentine." He looked over the car and gestured. "Go ahead."

"*Gracias,* officer," the driver said.

"Sorry for the delay," the officer said.

I said, "Don't worry about it, Sergeant. Have a great day."

The police officer waved at us as we pulled away and saluted with a smile. The driver merged into the nightmarish traffic. The driver said, "So, you're a doctor, huh? When I saw you, the first impression I had of you was that you were a Federale. I think the police officer must have thought the same, because he gave you a salute. You don't look like a doctor; you look like you're in the secret police. Did you see the respect he treated you with? Believe me, my friend, those guys don't treat everyone like that here."

I smiled and asked him, "*Te gustaria ganarte una buena lana?*[13] Five hundred dollars."

The driver's head jerked around abruptly to look at me with bulging eyes. "Sure. Who do I have to kill?"

I smiled. "No, you don't have to kill anybody. The only thing you have to do is take me to your garage." I leaned forward and rested my arms against the back of the front seat. I handed him a

---

[13] Do you want to make some good money?

small piece of paper with a taxi ID number on it. "I just want to talk to whoever drives this taxi cab. Can you arrange it?"

"Oh, I know you're the federal police now! My friend, with that look, you cannot fool anyone!"

I smiled. "I know." I removed my sunglasses and put a hand on the driver's shoulder. "What is your name?"

"Poncho."

"OK, Poncho. I'm many things, but I'm not a policeman. I give you my word of honor that somebody tried to kill me today at the airport. I want to talk to this guy to find out who sent them to do that."

Poncho stroked his chin in surprise. "Oh, my God! You are the guy in the airport? Oh, my God, please don't kill me! I've got eight kids." He began to perspire and crossed himself. "Maria, three; Paco, four; Felicita, five; Octavio, six…."

I squeezed his shoulder. "Stop it—calm down, I'm not going to hurt you. I'm not a murderer. I just want to find out why these people tried to kill me today. The people who died at the airport today are the actual murderers, and only two people, not ten. I was just defending myself."

Poncho crossed himself, kissed his fingers, and started to pray. He mumbled, "*Virgen de Guadalupe*, protect me."

I smiled again. "Remember, you can make your money and help me, but if you don't want to, you don't have to. No problem." I leaned back into my seat, shifting into a comfortable position.

Poncho breathed deeply. "Of course I want to help you. You don't have to pay me. This is for free. Don't worry about the $500. That way, you can see that I'm really your friend."

"I'm not going to pay you. I was just going to give you a good tip. If you do a really good job, it won't be a payment."

Poncho replied, "For me it will be a pleasure. I mean, someone tried to kill you, and for what reason? That's not right. The guy that drives that taxi always gets me in trouble. It will be a double pleasure for me." He picked up the radio receiver.

"OK, Poncho. Thank you. I really appreciate that."

Poncho motioned to his lips for silence as he spoke into the receiver. "Dispatcher, dispatcher, over."

"Yes, Poncho," an answering female voice said. "What do you need?"

"I have an old lady as a fare in my car. *Una norte Americana.*[14] The lady tells me she lost her passport and wallet in taxi number 00976."

"OK, no problem," the voice replied. "Bring her to the central station, and I will call the driver of 00976 to come in so that we can check the taxi."

"OK, we'll be there in fifteen or twenty minutes, depending on traffic. Over and out." Poncho replaced the receiver, turned to me and winked. He turned back forward and relaxed in his seat. "*Bien mi Jefe*[15]?"

"That is perfect, Poncho," I replied, putting my left hand on his shoulder. "Thank you very much. Since you don't want to charge me, I want to give you a little tip." I handed him a $100 bill.

He looked at it and said, "Wow!"

"Keep the change."

"Thank you, very much!" he exclaimed. "I can keep the change, no problem. But I still want to do you the favor you asked of me."

"Of course, my friend. That is worth a lot more than what I just gave you."

Poncho smiled in satisfaction. "This is not a little tip—it's a big one! Thank you, very, very much."

We drove into the garage of the taxi terminal. I said to him, "Leave me at the entry. When people ask you where the lady is, you tell them that she's in the restroom. Don't worry about me. I'll take care of the rest. You've already done your part. Forget about everything, and I'll probably see you again. So, see you soon."

"OK, *mi Jefe. Valla con dios.*"

"*Valla con dios, mi amigo,*" I replied.

Poncho smiled. "Good luck to you."

---

[14]   A North American
[15]   Is that OK, my boss?

I walked straight to the restrooms as Poncho slowly walked over to the tall chair in which his dispatcher sat, who was engrossed in some account ledgers. Instead of going into the restroom, I lingered just outside. I pulled out a collapsible spyglass and watched Poncho as he spoke with the dispatcher. Reading his lips, I was able to corroborate with satisfaction that Poncho did not compromise me as he told her that the North American lady was in the bathroom.

Taxi 00976 entered the garage. I immediately recognized the driver. He drove deep into the garage. I watched him as he wrapped his revolver in a small blanket and placed it in the seat as if it were a back rest. He opened all the doors to the taxi as Poncho and the dispatcher searched it. They found nothing, and so all of them returned to the dispatcher's office.

The dispatcher asked Poncho, "Where is the lady?" Poncho spread his hands, shrugged, and pointed at the restrooms as we had agreed. She walked over and went into the lady's room. Moments later she came back out with an expression of disappointment on her face. "There's nobody here," she reported.

I took this opportunity to rapidly sneak inside the taxi, which was positioned facing the restrooms. I snatched the revolver from where the driver had hidden it and put it in my outside jacket pocket. I concealed myself behind the driver's seat and pressed the button on my umbrella to snap the blade out. From that vantage, I watched everything through my spyglass, as the windshield was clear.

Poncho raised his arms in confusion. "I don't know where she went. She said she was going to the bathroom."

I smiled, feeling good about his loyalty.

The other taxi driver was obviously in a hurry to go. He said, "Well, there's nobody here to talk to, so I'm leaving."

He got into his cab and virtually burned rubber to get out of the garage. He came to a red light and stopped. The right rear door opened, and a tall, well-dressed, beautiful woman laden with shopping bags hopped into the back seat. Because of her dark sunglasses and packages, she could not see me.

"Take me to the American Embassy, *por favor,*" she directed. The driver turned to look at her and switched the meter on. The light turned green and he drove off. The woman arranged her packages and noticed me. I put my finger to my lips. I gestured with my knife blade to ensure her terrified silence. Slowly, I crept up to sit down next to her. I put the umbrella up to her, and she gasped.

The driver glanced up in his rearview mirror and desperately started to dig for his revolver. I leaned back and pointed the umbrella at him. Casually, I pulled his weapon out and put it on top of my leg in plain view.

I pointed at it. "Is this what you're looking for?"

He looked at me in panic through the rearview mirror. I'm fairly certain he was thinking of the two men he had seen me kill. He began to sob. "*Por favor,* I have six children. Please don't kill me. I don't have anything to do with those guys at the airport. I have that revolver only because so many people try to rob me."

It sounded rehearsed, like a child at play. It even had the sing-song quality of something he had memorized by rote. "Remember, there's a lot of robbers in this city," he continued, "and they always think we have a lot of cash. That's the only reason I have that gun. I don't intend any harm to anyone. I swear to you and I swear to God."

I looked at him in disbelief, remembering the two shots he fired at me. The woman was mute in her panic. She had no idea what was going on, clearly, and must have been regretting her choice of taxi at that moment. I understood her fear and looked her in the eyes.

"Don't worry," I said to her, "this has nothing to do with you. If you do what I ask of you, nothing will happen to you." I turned to the driver. "As for you—if what you say is true, and you do what I tell you, you might live to see those six children grow up. Keep calm and answer my questions. Take me someplace where we can talk. Don't try anything, or you know what will happen to you."

He accidentally swerved into the other lane. He noticed it and quickly corrected himself.

"Watch the road and pull yourself together," I said. I put the umbrella close to his neck. "You better drive straight and not attract any attention to yourself. If the police stop us, I will shove this blade through your neck."

"I swear to God, I'll do whatever you say, sir," the driver said.

"Whatever you say. I'll take you to a place where we can talk, don't worry."

"I will give both you guys my word of honor that nothing will happen to you if you do exactly as I tell you," I said.

The lady breathed a little more freely.

The driver crossed himself. "I swear to God on the health of my kids that I will do exactly what you say, and so will she. Is that not true, lady?"

She said, "Yes, there's no need to harm anyone. We will cooperate fully with you."

"OK," I said, "keep driving. Don't exceed the speed limit. We have a lot to talk about. Just behave like we're all a good family." I smiled as I realized they were acting this way because they were terrified.

As we drove through the crowded streets, I played with the blade on the umbrella by opening and closing it. Every time the blade sprang out, the driver twitched and jumped a little. I noticed the lady did not take her eyes off of either me or the blade. I examined her, from the exquisite, soft leather of her shoes to the salon-coiffed hairstyle she sported. I saw that she was doing exactly the same with me. She was even noticing the monograms on my socks as well as the rings on my hands, especially the blue topaz and diamond ring, which clearly had caught her attention.

I started to scrutinize her more closely. Her sunglasses were expensive, and the perfect manicure on her fingers must have cost a pretty penny. Her clothes were the latest in high fashion. She appeared to be either very wealthy or an aristocrat of the highest class. She removed her sunglasses and looked into my eyes.

"Who are you?" she asked. "What do you want? It's obvious money is not your objective. Your clothing, your watches, your rings—they are all extremely expensive. You're obviously not a criminal. Far from that."

I smiled and shook my head as I looked at her in silence. I unloaded the revolver. Bullets in one hand, I pointed the revolver towards the roof and pulled the trigger a few times. Every time the hammer clicked forward with a snap, the driver jumped a little. Then I patiently and slowly reloaded it.

I replied to her question, "I just returned from a nice but stressful trip to Cuba. I thought I would have a little peace and quiet for a few days, and let my adrenaline levels drop a little. I didn't plan to have any commotion or trouble. Those two guys at the airport took a shot at me and tried to kill me, only a little while ago." I pointed to my briefcase. "You see these two tears? Those are from the shooting. Thank God this case is bulletproof; otherwise these two holes would be holes in my head."

I pointed at the third and fourth tears in the corner. "These, however, came from this revolver." As I gestured with it, I casually tapped the muzzle against the driver's neck. "This gentleman here had it in the front seat. He claims to have nothing to do with it, and yet he shot at me two times. If I hadn't acted quickly to protect myself, I would be lying on a metal slab in the hospital with a tag on my toe at this moment."

I shifted slightly in my seat. "I will tell you something, Madame. I have been having a really bad day so far. Generally speaking, it started to get better once you stepped into this taxi. You bring some relaxation to my spirit. I have to ask myself: if all of this hadn't happened, would I have had the pleasure of meeting you?"

She smiled at me in slight confusion. Then in an irritated tone, she asked the driver, "Why did you shoot this man? Are you a cowboy, a Mafioso disguised as a taxi driver, or what?"

The driver jerked his head towards her.

I shoved the revolver into his neck. "Keep your eyes on the road. Don't look back here, dammit. What did I tell you before?"

The driver nervously complied. "Sir, I promise you, I acted only on impulse. I saw you shoot the man outside the taxi and then stab and kill the one inside, and I thought I was next. I was only trying to defend myself. I had no idea what was actually going on. I acted on impulse, not intentionally."

I held the briefcase up, and tapped the driver on the shoulder with it. "Not intentionally, huh? Those holes would be in my head if I hadn't acted quickly enough."

The driver started to sob like a baby unable to find its toy. I was extremely angry at this, but I controlled myself and remained calm. I sniffed the air and could tell that he had urinated himself slightly.

The young woman was more relaxed as she realized that what was going on had nothing to do with her. She held her hand out to me. "Zuyen is my name."

I put the briefcase down, switched the revolver to my left hand, and took her hand to kiss it. "I am Dr. Valentine."

"Oh! A doctor!"

"Yes, I am."

My hand still in hers, Zuyen said, "You have soft hands. I knew at once that you were some kind of professional, which is one of the reasons I determined that you weren't a common criminal. Your manners are likewise too refined."

My left hand raised up to rest the muzzle of the revolver against the sweating driver's neck. Zuyen crossed her beautiful legs. The slit in her dress exposed her beautiful brown skin. Through the window, I saw a place that looked ideal to stop.

"That is a good spot," I ordered. "Pull over."

Zuyen noticed my anger and said, "I don't want to pry into your business, Dr. Valentine, but have you considered the possibility that the driver was telling you the truth?"

I could see in the rearview mirror the driver's eyes widen in appreciation, as if he had heard the voice of an angel. I smiled.

Zuyen continued, "If you think about it, there's a strong possibility that he shot that revolver in self-defense because you had already killed two people. I don't know about you, but I would do the same in that position to protect myself."

I looked at her and nodded. "Yes. That is exactly what I want to find out. That is why I want to talk to him about those men he had in the taxi in a nice, quiet place. I hope in my heart that he is able to convince me that this is exactly the truth." I winked at her. The driver pulled over. We were now in the outskirts of Mexico City.

Zuyen asked the driver, "What is your name?"

The driver turned slowly because he felt the revolver still against his neck. "My name is José, *señorita. Mucho gusto*[16]."

Zuyen replied with a smile, "Oh, like Jesus' father. But the Joseph I know from the Bible didn't shoot at people."

José swallowed hard, not liking what he heard too much. "Yes, *señorita*, you are right in making that comparison." He crossed himself and put his head down in regret and shame. He began to sniffle and weep once more. "I beg that God will forgive me."

We had parked under some trees. I opened my door and said to José, "Get out of the car. Go sit down on the rock beneath that tree." I held out my hand. "Before you go, give me the keys to the car."

I tucked the revolver into my belt and trained the umbrella at the back of José's neck. We walked over towards the tree. As we walked, I said, "Here is an irony. If I kill you today, I will use the same revolver you tried to murder me with. As the Bible says, those who live by the sword die by the sword."

José put both hands to his face as he cried once more.

"Go and sit down right there and wait for me," I said. "Stop crying and be a man, for God's sake, like you were today when you shot at me."

José walked to the large rock about thirty feet away and sat down.

Zuyen had gotten out of the car and stood by it as she waited. I gestured for her to come over to me. When she got near enough, I said in a very low voice, "I need your help." She nodded. "I've already terrified him enough. He'll have to change his underwear, as I noticed his urine all over the car. I want you to go over to

---

[16]   It's a pleasure to meet you.

where he's sitting and tell him to calm down. Tell him that if he tells me the truth, he'll go home today. But if he lies to me, I'll kill him right here. Can you do that?"

Her eyes widened. "You're not going to hurt him, are you?"

"Don't worry. I'm no killer. But I need to find the truth here and discover who is behind all of this. That is the only way I can prevent another attempt. If I'm to find the string which leads me to that information, it is here today at this time."

Zuyen looked into my eyes once more to determine if I was in earnest. "I want to believe you. But it's hard, after knowing that you killed two men today."

I returned her intense look. I put my hand on her shoulder. "I give you my word of honor that he won't get hurt unless he tries something stupid."

She nodded and smiled. She put her hand on top of mine and patted it. "Those words comforted me earlier in the taxi: your word of honor. That gave me a feeling of peace, since I know that word doesn't exist in a criminal's vocabulary."

I smiled. "You are a very smart lady. Let's do this, please. The sooner we finish, the sooner I will be able to get you to the American Embassy."

She smiled at my remembering her destination.

"If you need a passport or anything expedited," I said, "maybe I can do a small service for you there."

She smiled again, but this time it was mischievously. It was also blended with curiosity, I noticed. However, I did not comment on it.

We started to walk over to where José was sitting, and she said, "Thank you for offering the aid of your friends in the embassy."

"You're welcome. It's nothing." I stopped walking. "I'm going to stay here. Signal to me when you think he's ready for me. Go ahead."

I stood a distance away while Zuyen spoke with him. After a bit she waved me over. I approached. José was still terrified of me, visibly shaking like a leaf.

I said, "OK, what can you tell me about your friends? Any detail could help me prevent another encounter over the next few days."

José's eyes widened. "No, no, no—they're not my friends. Please don't color it like that."

"OK, but you tried to defend them today, which is why I thought they were your friends."

José shook his head emphatically. "I already told you, man. I was just trying to defend myself. It was an impulse. A stupid impulse. I shouldn't have gotten involved. I'm a taxi driver. I'm not a professional killer. I don't make my living doing that. Why don't you want to believe me, man? Believe me, it wasn't my intention to shoot you. Thank God I didn't do any harm to you. Why won't you believe me?" He looked me straight in the face.

I slowly brought the umbrella up to José's forehead. His eyes widened, and he raised his hands up so high that he looked like he was trying to touch the sky. Zuyen crossed herself and looked away, which increased his terror.

I spoke slowly. "You know why I don't believe you, José?"

His eyes were fixed on me in panic, unblinkingly. Once more, I caught a whiff of fresh urine. "Why won't you believe me?" he repeated. "Why? Why? For the Virgin of Guadalupe, I implore you."

I shifted the umbrella down to his throat. He looked like he was on the verge of a nervous breakdown. I slowly, deliberately, moved my finger to the button. He knew what that meant, because of my repeated use of it in the car.

I said, "I can believe you are a taxi driver, a hardworking man. And would want to defend yourself against any common criminal who might want to assault you if you had a knife, baton, baseball bat, even a set of brass knuckles. But you don't have any of those. You have a revolver. Those who carry firearms do so because they are waiting for someone to try and kill them or are in immediate fear for their lives. If the criminal gets the revolver, he can use that to kill you."

He looked at me imploringly. I continued, looking him straight in the eyes. "You knew these men. What made you carry that revolver? Have you worked for them before? Have you driven them to commit these kinds of acts before? I'm not going to waste too much time with you. You have only a few seconds to answer truthfully, or you will lose your life, right here and now."

I had gone from a gentle, pleasant tone to one of command as I punctuated my points and anger by pressing the tip of the umbrella against his Adam's apple. I asked once more, "How many times have you driven these guys around, *cabrón*[17]? Tell me, or you die."

José screamed out, "No, no—please! It's true, I drive them." I moved the umbrella a little to the side and the blade snapped out close by José's face, cutting his cheek slightly. He began to cry once more. "OK, OK, please, stop it. I'll tell you everything."

"OK, you get a second chance. Start talking."

"Yes, yes, I know them. I'll tell you everything. What do you want to know?" He wiped his face and grew more panicked at the sight of his blood on his fingers.

"Sit down," I commanded. "How long have you known these guys, and where did they come from? Who were they?"

"They were Cuban, from the embassy."

"From the Cuban Embassy?"

"Yes, yes."

"You knew this all the time and yet you kept silent. You realize you're an accomplice?"

José tucked his hand inside his vinyl jacket to show me something, but I reacted quickly to put the blade against his throat.

"No, no—it's OK. I'm just getting something to show you." He pulled out his wallet and removed two business cards. He handed them to me.

One of them read, "Octavio Ramirez, Cultural Attaché, Cuban Embassy." The other card read, "Martin Gonzalez, Intercounsel, Cuban Embassy." Both cards had the crest of Cuba on them.

---

[17]   Damn it

I shook my head. "What did you have to do with these guys? What kind of work do you do with these people?"

"No sir, I don't work for the embassy. I'm just a taxi driver."

"You're starting to exhaust my patience, José," I said angrily. "How do you know these people? You just told me that you're more than just a driver. You said you drove them around many times."

José said in a frightened voice, "Sir, they paid me very well and gave me a huge tip for keeping my mouth shut. Every time they came into town they called me. They even had my private number. Whenever they had an assignment, they called me."

"Ah, ha! An assignment. What kind of assignment, and what kind of trips did you make with these guys? Where did you go? Why did you have to keep your mouth shut?"

He babbled, "Well, I took them to different places, the houses of Cuban families, different businesses. Sometimes I heard shots. I would read in the papers the next day that someone had been assassinated or killed."

With my left hand, I stroked my forehead. I pursed my lips in anger. "I see, I see. So, in other words, you took these assassins to the houses of innocent people, who were probably fleeing from persecution in Cuba, and Castro sent these people to kill them for whatever reason."

"God forgive me, sir," he said, "I was only the driver."

"Yeah, you were the driver, but you are also an accomplice. You are an accessory to the murder of people whose only 'crime' was fleeing Castro's horrors with their families. Perhaps for political reasons, or because they left illegally, they send these assassins to Mexico and other places in the world to punish them. How can you live with that on your conscience, driving these assassins to their murder locations, and then go home to your six children with the filthy money you earned and the blood of these innocent lives on your hands?"

José stared at the ground, tears in his eyes. I was utterly shocked how José could be so easily converted into being an accessory to such monstrosities. "When did you become the accomplice to murderers for a handful of pesos?"

José put his face in his hands. "God forgive me. When I saw you kill both of them this afternoon, you enlightened me and poked my conscience. I realize now and firmly believe that God sent you to punish them, as well as me. I was scared then, and now I'm going to die for doing these bad things without remorse before."

I looked at him in pity now. I thought to myself how low people could sink for something as inconsequential as money. "How many people, José? How many were killed on these trips?"

He remained staring at the ground. "I don't know, sir. I've been driving them for years."

I restrained myself from slapping him silly as my anger burned once more in my breast. I removed the umbrella from his neck and tapped it against my leg. I stroked my beard with my other hand as I sat down next to him on the rock. He shifted to make room for me.

"You're not going to die today. Not today. I know you were one more victim of those assassins. I think you will have enough punishment for the rest of your life from your conscience. If you didn't drive them, someone else would have, especially as you told me they paid you a lot of money for it. Did you ever kill anyone?"

José jumped at that. "No, no, no—I didn't even know for certain what they did. I heard the shots and read about it in the paper, so I assumed that's what they did." He crossed himself. "But I never killed anyone myself."

I nodded in satisfaction and smirked. "Maybe I saved you today, after all. If you had shot me today in the airport, you would have gone to Hell without any chance of salvation. I'm an innocent bystander, so you had no reason to defend yourself."

He crossed himself once more and kissed his hand. "Forgive me, sir. Forgive me. I tell you this from the bottom of my heart. I will never hold a firearm in my hand again. I swear to you before God. When I drove away, I thanked God a thousand times that I didn't hurt you. I saw you standing there in my rearview mirror and thanked God many times that I missed." He crossed himself again.

I could see that he was genuinely repentant, both in voice and attitude. His remorse was sincere. "What is your last name, José?"

"José Angel Gonzales Martinez, sir," he said with a little pride. I pulled a small tape recorder out of my coat pocket. "José, I need your help, even though I have everything you just said recorded here. I promise nobody will hurt either you or your family."

"Are you going to arrest me, sir?" he asked fearfully. "Are you a policeman? Do you work for Interpol?"

"No, José—I'm not a policeman. I'm just a freedom fighter. And no, I'm not going to arrest you."

He looked at me distrustfully. "I asked because you're dressed like a policeman and have all these weapons, and now you have a tape recorder."

I shook my head with a slight smile. "I just want you to tell me something. I don't want to get you more involved than you already are, but my friends might need confirmation when I play this tape. No judge, no policeman, you understand? Just my friends."

José nodded. "Yes, I understand."

"If I need you to, you will repeat the same thing to my friends—just my friends. You understand?"

"Your friends?"

"Yes, José—just my friends."

"OK, my friend," José said.

"Thank you, José. It's good to know that I can count on you, that if I need to take you anywhere to talk to my friends, I can find you and you won't hide from me. I don't ever want to put this umbrella to your throat again. That gives me a great sense of relief. God will reward you. Being involved in these horrible things might actually lead to your salvation by doing this good. Perhaps God has given you this opportunity to redeem yourself for your bad actions."

José clasped his hands prayerfully. "Redemption. Thank you."

"Yes," I said. "Redemption. You have to thank God for this. If somebody else were in my shoes, you might not be given this opportunity. I assure you of that." I held my hand out to him. "Do we have a deal, José?"

He clutched my hand with both of his. "Yes, my friend. We have a deal. Thank you for letting me redeem myself!"

"You might have a great reason for being alive. We might be able to put a stop to what these people have been doing these past years."

"Yes, yes, OK sir. I will help you with whatever you need. I will be at your service, unconditionally. I swear to God." He crossed himself again.

Zuyen walked closer to us, having heard the entire conversation. She said to José, "There is always more satisfaction to being on the side of good than on the side of evil. Nothing, even the greatest golden treasures, brings you more suffering, trouble, and death than when it comes from evil hands. Good will always bring you tranquility, happiness, and greatness."

José pulled a business card out of his wallet and handed it to Zuyen. "Thank you, lady. If you ever need me for anything, call me, day or night. I will be there for you."

Zuyen looked at me. I could see from her misty eyes that she felt pity for José following his display of emotion. José added, "My pager is on the back of the card. If you call me, I will drop whatever I'm doing to come and help you." He pulled out another card, handed it to me, and repeated his offer.

The three of us walked back to the taxi. José trotted ahead to open Zuyen's door for her. After he closed it, he ran around to open mine, but I stopped him. "You don't have to do that, José, but thank you. It's good for the lady, but I'm fine."

José smiled. "I do it with pleasure, sir. Where are we going?"

Zuyen and I said simultaneously, "The American Embassy." We looked at each other curiously.

José mumbled, "Of course, of course. Right away."

Chapter 5

THE ASIAN ROMANCE

US Embassy in Mexico City,
Main Entrance

US Embassy Rear Entrance

José started the engine and drove off towards our destination. Zuyen and I exchanged another glance, this time much more at ease. Our relief, however, was nothing compared to José's. Zuyen and I felt as if we had formed a bond through the experience we had just shared.

It started to grow dark, and the full moon shone down on us. José asked, "Do you guys mind if I put some music on the radio?"

I looked at Zuyen as I shrugged.

She said, "Well, it depends on what you want to play. No mariachi music, please."

"Don't worry about it, *señorita,* I have wonderful taste in music."

"No, I didn't say that music was bad," she replied. "I'm just not in the mood for it."

"Let me play a tape I made myself."

"OK," Zuyen said. "Let's see how good your taste in music is." The tape was a blend of jazz, flamenco, and Polynesian instrumental music. Zuyen and I exchanged surprised looks.

Zuyen said, "Very pleasant and relaxing music, José."

I said, "You surprised us, José. Excellent!"

"Thank you," José said. "I told you I have good taste in music. I myself play the trumpet."

We all smiled as we drove on. A little while later, we arrived at the embassy. We all got out, and José, Zuyen, and I each shook hands. I tried to give José his revolver back, wrapped in the blanket, but he refused.

"No, no—I made a promise to God," he said. "You keep it. I will have nothing to do with guns anymore."

I smiled and put my hand on his shoulder. Zuyen and I walked up to the gates of the embassy. The guards opened the gates and greeted her.

One said, "*Buenas noches*[18], *señorita* Zuyen."

She replied, "Hello. *Como estas*[19]?"

"Fine," he replied.

She nodded in my direction. "He is with me."

We walked through the beautiful gardens. I started to wonder who she was. Clearly, the guard knew her quite well, and she must have a certain authority for me to be passed through without showing any identification. She smiled as if she knew something I didn't.

"Do you work here?" I asked.

She smiled again. "Follow me, please."

---

[18]   Good evening
[19]   How's it going?

She opened a door. More guards saluted us as we entered. Once more, no questions were asked. She was walking through the embassy as if she were the owner.

She asked me, "Who did you want to speak with?"

"The ambassador or his assistant."

"It's kind of late," she said. "I don't think the ambassador will be available, but let's see what I can do."

She took me to a side parlor with a refrigerator and a bar. She opened it and asked, "Would you like something to eat or drink?"

"Actually, I haven't eaten all day. The Cuban airline only provided us a tiny juice and nothing else. If you have a glass of fruit juice and some crackers, I would appreciate that very much." I checked one of my watches. "Oh, my God! It's already nine o'clock!"

She pulled a large jar of orange juice out of the refrigerator and poured us each a glass. She filled a bowl of nuts. She took a sip of her orange juice and grabbed a handful of nuts. We sat down at the bar.

She popped a few nuts into her mouth. "Whatever you have to say to the ambassador—is it so important that it cannot wait? As you've observed, it's so late that I don't think he'll be in a disposition to take an appointment now."

My face was somber. "Zuyen, if you could get in touch with the ambassador, I would really appreciate it. I need to speak with him as soon as possible. It's a matter of national security. Tell him, if you can, that if he can find some time for me, I have an intelligence report and identification to give to him."

Zuyen looked at me in surprised wonderment. She gulped. "OK, let me see what I can do. I will try to get in touch with him at once."

We finished our juice and looked at each other admiringly. I certainly felt a spark, and her smile seemed to indicate that she might be going beyond simply regard for me. There was a mutual attraction here. She stood up and walked behind me. As she did, she patted my shoulder and gave it a slight squeeze. I turned to look at her, and our eyes met.

Before she left, I said, "You know, you have the most beautiful eyes I've ever seen in a woman. They are not only sweet and beautiful, they are also classy and elegant."

"Thank you," she replied. "Your eyes aren't too bad, either. They're very kind and sincere. You smell very good, and from what little I know about you, you are an extraordinary man."

I took her hand and pulled her in to me. I gave her a tender kiss on the lips.

"Wow!" she breathed. "Do you believe in love at first sight?"

"Yes," I answered.

"Me, too."

I moved towards her to kiss her once more, but she halted me by placing a delicate hand on my chest. "Not here." She pointed to the cameras.

I smiled. "I understand."

She caressed my beard. "Let me try to get the ambassador for you." I breathed deeply. She smiled and said, "That was a very sweet kiss. I've never had one like that before in my life."

"Thank you," I replied. "But yours is sweet and sour, just the way I like it."

She smiled once more. "I guess that is good."

"Not good—it's great and delicious."

We looked at each other longingly for a few seconds. Then I pulled out my briefcase and opened it. I pulled out a sealed envelope with large red letters which read, *Personal and Confidential: Top Secret.* "This envelope should be in the U.S.A. tonight. Not tomorrow morning. Tonight! It's extremely important. People's lives depend on this envelope. Please convince the ambassador to put it in the diplomatic mail *tonight.*"

She could not hold back her curiosity any longer. She looked me in the eyes and asked, "Who are you?" No sooner had she asked that than she placed a finger on her lips. "Never mind. It's not important who you are or what your name is. Let me go and see what I can do for you."

A great deal of time passed, and I was growing impatient. It seemed like hours had passed after that adrenaline-filled day. I looked down the corridor and saw two Marines just outside the door through which Zuyen had disappeared. They were armed with M-4 carbines. They hadn't been there when we had entered, so I was uncertain what their purpose there was now. I sat down, poured more juice, and ate some nuts. I looked at the wall and saw the portrait of Bill Clinton, the current president of the United States. I picked up my briefcase in one hand and my umbrella in the other, preparing myself for possible action. I had no idea who this woman was in reality, and the monkeys of distrust jumped inside my brain. Was she another spy? Was this a setup? I began to perspire, though I couldn't tell if it was from stress or the ambient temperature of the room.

The door opened abruptly. The two Marines entered. The first one asked, "Are you Dr. Valentine, sir?"

"Yes, may I help you?"

"The ambassador will be with you in ten minutes, sir. He asked us to please apologize to you, but he is in the middle of a party now. As soon as he can leave his guests, he'll be in to see you, sir."

"No problem," I said. "Please tell the ambassador for me that the night is still young, as am I. I can wait a little longer."

The Marine smiled, saluted, and left. They closed the door behind them. A great release swept over me like a shower, clearing the monkeys out of my brain. Still holding the attaché by my side, I sat down in a comfortable chair, this time facing the door. I picked up a magazine from the stand, and flipped through the pages. A few minutes later, a man of about 5'10" in his late fifties, gray-haired and with a trimmed white beard entered. He was very well-dressed. He came over to me, his hand extended.

"I am Ambassador Robert Budrous. Dr. Valentine?"

I took his hand. "Yes. It's a pleasure to meet you. I'm sorry to wake you at this late hour." We shook hands and sat down. "Mr. Ambassador, I've brought you some extremely important documents."

He put a hand on my shoulder. "Stop for a moment, please." He put a finger over his mouth and pointed at the cameras. "Follow me."

We stood up and left the room together. He saluted the Marines. As we walked, he said in a low voice, "The security system installed here is supposed to be for our protection. But today, we have to be careful because that same technology can be used against us. Any twelve-year-old boy could intercept our conversation, put it on the Internet, and create international gossip. That would destroy the careers of a lot of valuable people who have great intentions. I always take precautions. There's no respect for secrecy anymore, so I have my own conference room for private discussions. There are no cameras, recording equipment, not even electricity in there. Only candles."

We exchanged smiles, and the Marines followed us closely as we walked down the corridor. We came to a door, and he opened it. We walked into a conference room. He said, "I miss the old times without all this technology. I never feel secure anymore. By the way, don't call me 'Mr. Ambassador.' Call me Robert."

"OK, Robert," I replied with a grin.

Robert asked, "Is Valentine really your name?" He put his hand up. "No, you don't have to answer that. It's OK. You've made a great impression with Zuyen. You didn't actually get me out of anything important—I was at a diplomatic gathering. I was rather glad when she called me on my private phone and said that it was important enough for me to see you right away. I just had to find a way to excuse myself and leave the party."

He lit some candles around the conference room table. We sat down, and I placed my briefcase on the table. He said, "I see by your case that you had a rough day today." His fingers traced the gouges left by the bullets.

I shook my head sadly. "Yes, sir. Those marks aren't supposed to be there. They were meant to be in my head. Thanks to that case, I'm still alive."

He shook his head and looked at me. "Yes, Zuyen told me all about it. My God—you're a very lucky man, or you have some divine protection."

"Yes, I seriously believe that, and more even than that."

I opened the briefcase and pulled out some papers. Robert looked at me curiously. I removed a black notebook, some more paper, and a pen. I jotted some numbers on a slip of paper and handed it to him.

"I need a telephone with a secure line," I told him. "I need you to call either my contact O'Brien or his superior, Addison. The code word is 'The Lightning.' If you'll excuse me, I need to report what occurred in the airport."

"Of course. It was all over the news. One man died in the airport, shot in the head."

I started writing some notes. As I wrote, I replied, "Not one. Two."

"Oh!" He opened the door and spoke to the Marines outside. "Please go to my office and bring me a secure phone."

"Aye, aye, sir," replied the Marine. A few moments later, a polite knock on the door heralded the arrival of a small boxlike receiver unit.

Robert picked up the receiver and dialed the number I gave him. A woman's voice picked up on the other end. "Routing, please," she inquired.

Robert said, "25, 7, 14."

The woman's voice said, "Host name, please."

"Addison or O'Brien."

He was placed on hold, and then someone answered. "This is O'Brien. Who is this?"

"Yes, this is Robert Budrous, the U.S. Ambassador to Mexico. Pardon my call at this late hour."

"Yes, Mr. Ambassador. How can I help you? Don't worry about the time. When it's important, we're at your service 24/7."

Robert replied, "I have Dr. Valentine here."

"Yes? What is the code?"

"The Lightning."

"OK, sir. Can you put him on the phone, please?" Robert handed the phone to me with a nod. I took the phone as I continued to write.

"Are you OK?" O'Brien asked.

"Yes, everything is OK, and I'm fine. Just something unexpected at the airport, nothing I couldn't handle."

"Yes, we saw the news. We already figured out it had something to do with you. We were a little concerned. Too much exposure. Are you sure you're not hurt?"

"No, no—I'm fine. Not a single scratch. I have something that is extremely important. It is imperative that I stay in Mexico for a few nights. I will explain later. I will transmit to you a package the ambassador will send. It is important that you look into this immediately."

"But we were expecting you tonight."

"Yes, I know. There is something I have to do here, and it's deadly important. The package is safe. I've already taken care of the details."

"All right," O'Brien said. "Take care of yourself, and keep me informed."

"We are going to put it in the diplomatic mail tonight." I turned to Robert. "Right, Robert?" He nodded his head. "Yes, it will be on jet tonight. I put a note in the package that explains why I have to remain here."

"Yes, sir," he said. "I understand."

"I have to resolve this problem before I leave Mexico."

"OK. Take care of yourself." O'Brien sounded more relaxed. "Let me speak with the ambassador so I can make things easier for you in the capital."

I smiled. "Thank you, my friend. I'll see you soon."

O'Brien chuckled. "Let's hope we see you in one piece."

I handed the phone to Robert with a smile on my face. I continued to write. When I was finished, I slipped the note inside the envelope. I sealed all four borders of the envelope with red silicon sealant. I waved the envelope to speed the drying process. I touched it gingerly to make certain was dry and handed it to Robert.

Robert was telling O'Brien, "Yes, you can be sure that it will arrive later this morning." He hung up. He looked at me and said,

"OK, they're waiting for us at the airport. Let's go deliver this package."

We exited the conference room. The Marines followed us until we left the building. A Lincoln limousine waited for us with two men in civilian clothing. They opened the doors for us. A black Lincoln sedan pulled up to follow us. Inside it were four men armed to the teeth.

Robert asked me with a smile, "Are you really a doctor, or is this part of your cover?" He raised a hand. "I'm sorry—typical human curiosity. I know better than that and that these things are confidential." I smiled and looked at him. "I think it must be interesting. People like to see it in the movies, but no one would like to experience the danger personally. Your life must be one continual adrenaline rush, not knowing if you'll wake up in the morning. It must take a certain kind of person to do what you do." He smiled and waited quietly for an answer.

I looked at him for a second as the car drove through the city. The lights shone through the tinted, bulletproof windows. Robert looked disappointed at my continued silence. He pushed a button, and a bar unfolded near the center of the dividing window. "What would you like to drink?"

I answered, "A juice is fine."

"What do you prefer?" asked Robert as he opened the mini fridge. "I have orange or grapefruit."

"Either one. Both are my favorites."

He smiled. "They are my favorite juices, too!"

"I see we have a lot in common," I commented.

Robert put some ice in a glass and poured. "What did you mean by that?"

"Well, with all due respect, you have a beautiful wife. I loved my lady for so many years, but they killed her when they were trying to kill me. This broke my heart for a long while. I guess I won't find that kind of love again." I looked out through the window at the neon lights of businesses going by as I thought about Sandra.

Robert handed me a glass. "OK. I understand your pain. You loved her very much, eh?"

"Yes. She was one of my first loves. We'd known each other since we were eight years old. It sounds kind of depressing, eh?"

"No, no—I truly know how you feel," he said. "I lost mine in Vietnam."

"In Vietnam? What were you doing there?"

"I worked in the embassy in Saigon when they gave the orders to evacuate. My wife was coming through town on a motorcycle. I kept telling her not to do that, that we had Jeeps and armored vehicles. She ignored me and thought that she could blend in well. Right before my eyes, they took her away from me."

His eyes filled with tears. He took a bottle of Grand Marnier from the bar and poured it into his orange juice. He took a sip. "As she was approaching the embassy, I could see her. Then I saw some Viet Cong fighting some of our soldiers across the street. One of the Cong had a bazooka on his shoulder getting ready to fire. Just as she passed by them, he launched the missile." He took a large drink from his glass.

He was about to put the bottle away, but I held my glass out to him. He handed the bottle to me, and I topped my orange juice off with Grand Marnier. We raised our glasses and toasted.

Robert said, "Let's toast the stupidity of humans killing each other without reason. Now we're friends with China, who were the architects behind Vietnam. They sent their military advisers to the Viet Cong to arm the North Vietnamese against the south. They were responsible for the slaughter of hundreds of thousands of civilians and young people, and now we sit around the table with them and eat Russian caviar. We forget all the emotion associated with that killing. It's pathetic, but it's diplomacy and politics. We are all thinking optimistically that we will fix this world eventually."

He raised the envelope I had given him. He said sarcastically, "If you want, you can reopen this envelope and tell your friends that the ambassador of Mexico may no longer be suitable for this job. Tell them how angry I am by policy made through corruption."

I leaned back and observed Robert. He looked slightly embarrassed, as if he had said too much. He knew what line of work I was in, and reconsidered that it might not have been completely appropriate.

I smiled and said, "I understand. Sometimes I feel the same way. I don't work for the CIA. I work *with* them, along with different intelligence groups in the world. I don't have to tell them anything I don't think is appropriate. I only tell them what I think is appropriate and will save innocent lives. I don't get my hands dirty in the muddy waters of politics."

He smiled and took another sip. "By the way, Zuyen is not my wife. She's my daughter. If you ever decide to report our conversation, please leave her out of it. She thinks completely differently. She's too young. She's an innocent virgin in this filthy, nasty business. She's more like her mother, who never saw any flaw in anything we did. I don't want to tell her that her mother died for nothing. She prefers to think that her father is a hero and that her mother died as a hero for democracy." He shook his head and took another drink.

I was extremely pleased to hear that Zuyen was his daughter and not his wife. Robert noticed my smile. "What?" he asked.

I leaned back in my seat and took the envelope from his hand. I pressed my fingers around it as I thought about how many lives that envelope represented and how many had died for it. I said very sincerely, "'Respect for the rights of others is peace.' Those were the words of the great Mexican patriot, Benito Juarez."

The ambassador touched his beard in thought.

"I respect your opinions deeply," I continued. "Sometimes we are completely disappointed with the decisions of our leaders, including our own president. How many stupidities and mistakes have been made in the past year? They all hide themselves behind patriotism and freedom.

"For example, John F. Kennedy was responsible for many thousands of young Cuban and American lives, but he would not accept responsibility for his decisions. What do we remember today of the Bay of Pigs? An invasion of the American government on Cuban soil. In actuality, the ones who died were the Cubans and a few Americans. They never remember these people as great patriots who risked their freedom and lives to protect democracy around the world. People will only remember that the United States government attacked a foreign country, which is utterly ridiculous. All the United States did was promise to back up these young patriots only to abandon them to their own luck without food, ammunition, or water.

"Let me tell you something: I never blamed the United States government for it. You have to be completely ignorant to not personally blame JFK and his administration for it. I will never be an agent for the CIA, and I will never receive a pay check from any government. If I did, then I would have to do what they order me to do. There's a big difference between working *with* you and working *for* you. That is the question: to be or not to be."

Robert looked at me in surprise and touched the envelope with his hands. "Wait a minute. You want to tell me that you're risking your life to get this information to the CIA, and you're not getting paid? You're not an agent?"

"The answer to both questions is no. I'm not bringing it to the CIA. I'm bringing it to people above the CIA. And I'm not getting paid to do it. That is the arrangement I have with them. You don't even have an idea how many lives it cost to get this out of Cuba, nearly including my own today at the airport. There's not enough money to pay for what anybody does in this kind of business, even those who do get paid for it."

Robert looked at me in admiration. "So, you're not part of the CIA, then. I can't believe it!"

I said proudly, "No. I don't know what O'Brien told you, but I'm a freedom fighter. What I do I do for decency, for my principles, and for the right of men to be free. I promised myself when I left Cuba that I would spend the rest of my life preventing innocent people from fighting and dying for something that is only a big fabrication designed to steal from people a decent way of living. People have the right to know what is going to happen when they follow these imbeciles. I will try until the last day of my life to influence and teach people how their ignorance in following such false promises can lose them their freedoms. That way, no other country will turn into what Cuba is today.

"I suffered a great deal in my youth in a psychological and physical jail. Cuba today is an illusion. Like Hollywood, it shows you the beauty of the buildings, but never the opportunity to look backstage to see the two by fours and rusty nails and extreme ugliness behind the façade. They portray beauty to the poor who think are they going to be helped. All that is just bull and lies. I am fighting to prevent that from happening to any other country."

Robert reached over and squeezed my shoulder. He gave me a look of approval. He picked up his glass and poured some more Grand Marnier into it. He offered me another glass.

"Now I realize why Zuyen has so much admiration for you after only meeting you a few hours ago," he said. "You are a very different man—no doubt about it. You are extremely passionate, and she thinks from your point of view."

I shook my head in disagreement. "I'm just one person trying to do the right thing."

Robert shook his head, as well. He smirked and said, "I don't think anybody else, including me, has the physical capacity to do what you've been doing."

I smiled. "You won't know until you try. You might be better than me. Sometimes we surprise ourselves."

Robert shook his head. "No, no, my friend—I know my limitations, and I know for a fact that I couldn't do even half of what you do."

I smiled once more and shook my head as well. "Well, maybe it's a gene I have that makes it come so naturally, as if I've done this in a past life. Members of my family have died in the fight for freedom in Cuba over the last hundred years. Sometimes I even have to ask myself what the point of it all is. By the way, the answer to your previous question is yes. I am a doctor—I'm a geneticist. I graduated from the Veterinary School in Rancho Boyeros. I continued my studies and got my PhD in genetics. My name, and I will be completely truthful with you, is Julio Antonio del Mármol. But to you, to anyone else, I'm Dr. Valentine. No exceptions to that rule."

He smiled. "Even Zuyen?"

"Well, we can make an exception for her."

Robert said, "I don't even know what we're fighting for anymore. We sit at the table with our enemies, like that Cuban regime, and sometimes we treat our friends like enemies. It's difficult to discern the ideological lines we follow these days. Political leaders apparently don't have any backbone, or they don't know what side they're really on."

I smiled and replied, "I'll tell you what. Anyone who crosses the line to kill innocent people, regardless of what political ideology they represent, have become my enemies. There are many other ways to resolve disagreements without killing innocents. That is why I don't follow some political leaders, even if they're supposedly on our side. I follow the Golden Rule: what is right is right, and what is wrong is wrong.

"We should embrace a leader for being the man he is and the principles he holds, not because of his party or the way he conducts himself publicly. Sometimes we think we have a leader who is on our side, and he winds up being the exact opposite. I think on some occasions that we have plants inside our friends. Sometimes they simply do things for their own political and personal interests. Let me tell you something from my point of view, Robert—we will be doing this until the end of our lives."

The ambassador looked at me in shocked surprise. I smirked and shook my head. "I expect that whatever we say here stays here, just as I expect you are the type of man I can call my friend. I sympathize with you, and I think we look at things the same way."

Robert looked at me and shook his head. "Dr. Mármol, or Dr. Valentine, or whatever your name is—to me, that's not important." He held out his hand to me. "You have a friend here." He smiled again. "Thank you for your confidence. I think we will not just be great friends; we will be great allies in the future. Sincerity and truth are the basis for a great, healthy friendship."

I gave him a half smile. "You're forgetting the most important one of the triad: loyalty." I took the envelope and slowly slid it over to the ambassador's hand as our limo arrived at the airport. We looked at each other with a shared sense of admiration and respect. I stroked my neck with my right hand. "I need to get in touch with the president of this country immediately."

Robert glanced at me. "I think I can help you with that. I'm a personal friend of his."

I thought about that for a second. "You are, eh? I have my own contacts here, and I would rather this information get to him from a different source than the American embassy. However, even though I had not considered this option before, it could be a great one if you two are personal friends. How close are you guys?"

"I'm very close to him. I can come to him as a friend, not just as the American ambassador."

I rubbed my fingers around the center of my forehead, thinking about that for a few seconds.

Robert watched me and added, "For your peace of mind, the kind of friendship I have with the president goes back many years. It's based on loyalty and honesty; we respect each other very much. He has great integrity as a man of high caliber and strong convictions."

I looked at him once more and nodded. "I think you can help me then. After all, God put us together for an important reason. You have no idea, but you're probably about to save the life not just of your friend, but of his entire family – not to mention preserving the stability of the region."

He looked at me with a blend of curiosity and concern. He put his right hand on my shoulder. "We will talk about this on the way back."

The limousine stopped, and the bodyguards opened the doors. We got out of the car and stood beside it. Four men stepped from the airplane and walked towards us. The plane was unmarked. The ambassador put the envelope into his briefcase, and locked it. He scrambled the numbers on the combination lock and handcuffed it to one of the four men. He leaned over and whispered something in the man's ear. He stepped away and the man saluted him in military fashion.

The other three men surrounded the one with the briefcase and escorted him to the ladder leading into the jet. He climbed aboard, and the ladder raised up. The three men returned to us as the aircraft rapidly took off, and we soon lost sight of it over the horizon. We got back into the limo and sat down.

Robert said, "OK, my friend, our mission is done. I hope your expectations are met on the other end of the line. Let's hope they don't sit on your information too long and instead move quickly on it."

I smiled and shook my head. "Yes, I hope so. Our objectives are not always met on the other end of the line, though."

Chapter 6

THE DIPLOMATIC ALLIANCE

As we drove back, Robert asked in a very curious tone, "Valentine, is the president's life really in danger?"

I looked at him grimly. "I'm afraid so, my friend. Not just extreme danger; I hope that I'm not too late and that our enemies aren't a step ahead. The Cuban government has no intention of letting someone create a real democracy, a Garden of Eden of freedom in Mexico. Their mission is to destroy democracy around the world, and they're not about to let a semi-socialist country flourish with it.

"You have to remember that Mexico is the only country that never broke diplomatic relations with Cuba, no matter how much pressure different U.S. presidents exerted on the presidents of Mexico over the years. Even with the embargo, Mexico is the only country in the Americas that maintained uninterrupted commercial ties with that communist island all these years. This new president, your friend, doesn't look with friendly eyes at that Cuban regime. The past presidents have been utterly self-serving, looking to their own profit in Cuba. You just told me your friend is a man of principles. That doesn't go along with the Castro brothers or the rest of their entourage over there. That briefcase we just shipped contains the proof of the entire assassination plot that's already in motion to take out not just your friend but his entire family."

The ambassador looked at me in shock. "Oh, my God! What you've been carrying with you all this while is a time bomb!"

I smiled and patted my briefcase. "You don't even know, my friend, how true your words are. What I've given you is a pipe bomb, but what I have in here is a nuclear bomb. We don't have too much time. We have to move quickly. I should have headed directly to the United States with this information, but it won't reach critical mass for perhaps a few months. What you have there, however, will happen soon if we don't stop it now. That's why I decided to stop here for a couple of days; it's equally important, but much more time sensitive."

Robert replied, "I can arrange a private meeting with the president immediately. I'll let you know in the morning when we're meeting with him." He gave me a worried look. "Now I know why they've tried to kill you."

The phone in the limo rang, interrupting the conversation. Robert picked up the phone. "Yes? Oh, yes—it's possible. Oh— asparagus and hollandaise sauce, shrimp fricassee with fresh pimentos and pineapple and wild rice? Mmmm! Don't say anything more, you've already got me hungry!" He rubbed his stomach. "We'll be there shortly. OK, I love you, too."

He hung up and looked at me. With a smile, he said, "That was Zuyen. I guess you told her you hadn't eaten all day. She knows it's a little late and unusual, but she won't take no for an answer. She's waiting for us at home with a wonderful meal." He raised his hand. "Don't decline it, OK? It's not an imposition—this is an invitation." He put his hand on my shoulder. "You must have made a great impression on her. She doesn't cook often, but when she does, she cooks like an army of angels."

I said no word but smiled in embarrassment. Robert said, "Since you'll probably stay in Mexico for a little while, you can use my guest cottage during your time here."

I shook my head. "Thank you, very much. I'm very grateful for your offer. But that really is unnecessary, and this time I don't want to impose."

"For your security, my friend, this is the safest place you can sleep in the city," he said.

After a moment, I said, "On second thought, given what happened today at the airport, I think it would be a great relief pertaining to my security."

"I know you're a smart man. I like you, and your decision pleases me very much. Meeting people like you once in a while restores my faith in human beings. I lost that some time ago in my line of work—dealing with traitors, politicians, and liars. This is no longer diplomacy. This is a battle of who plays the game better. Evidently, in these people's mind, whoever is the biggest liar wins."

I shook my head with a sad smile. "I don't like to be sarcastic, but you're very close to the truth. Unless you like to get in the mud with the pigs, you had better learn to play the game right so that you're never caught with your pants down. That can truly be embarrassing."

This time, Robert smiled sadly. "I have a thing or two to learn from you as a spy. It should be easy for me to arrange a quick meeting. I'll tell the president he will receive the information from the freedom fighters, not from the American embassy or any other source in intelligence. That way, he will feel more comfortable. I want to get him away from his entourage, so that whatever decision he makes will not be influenced by anyone around him. We have to consider that someone around him might a double agent."

"Very good thinking," I approved with a short laugh. "And you say you could never be a spy. You're playing this game like a professional already!"

I opened my briefcase and removed some documents, sorting through some pictures. I handed the photos to the ambassador. I pulled out a small tape recorder and handed him the earphones. "The important part begins after the Cuban music."

I press the play button on the recorder, and he flipped through the photographs as he listened to the recording. I watched his face change color in shock as he continued to listen and flip through the pictures. After about fifteen minutes, he removed the headset and looked at me with disturbed eyes. "This is unbelievable!" he exclaimed. "How did you get this out of Cuba?"

"The question is not how I got it out of Cuba," I answered. "The question is how we can protect the president's life without revealing to anyone where I obtained that information and the sources inside Cuba that provided it. That data is more valuable than anything else I have here in this briefcase, not only for the future but also to maintain the flow of that information uninterrupted. For that reason, I would rather die than tell anyone where it came from, without exception."

I put the recorder back in my briefcase. "That's why, when you mentioned your friendship with the president, I realized how important you could be. If you vouch for me one hundred percent, there will be no doubt in his mind that this information is completely truthful and valid, and then he won't need any proof to follow my suggestions. It will make it easier for me to protect him and his family. After he hears and sees this information, it won't go to any other agency in the Mexican government, because I will destroy it in order to protect my sources in Cuba. That is my responsibility."

He smiled and tapped the briefcase. "Have you taken into consideration that someone could take this from you by force?"

I smirked. "I've taken that into consideration already, yes. There's a small electronic device, a remote control. If this briefcase ends up in the wrong hands or I see myself in a situation which could jeopardize that information, I will blow it up with everyone around it. I would rather do that than to allow it to fall into the hands of my enemies. I would rather show this firsthand to the president before I'm forced to do that. Believe me, my enemies won't stop at anything. If they have to blow up you, me, this city, the entire world, they will. They don't want their cover blown, especially over something as tremendous as assassinating the president of this country or a bigger bombshell: a direct attack designed to kill thousands of people on U.S. soil."

I patted the briefcase. "However, I don't want to distract you with this other terrorist plot. We should concentrate on preserving the stability of the region and the security of the president and his family. That, right now, should be our priority."

Robert shook his head and clicked his tongue. "So, I was right on the money when I said that it was a time bomb. Sometimes we say things that are close to the truth and we don't even know it. Did you want to put your briefcase in a safe in the embassy?"

"I really appreciate your offer, but this briefcase has to be with me and sleep with me as if it were my wife. Even if my wife and I were to have a fight, we have to work it out in order to sleep together. No separation is allowed."

The limo stopped at a security checkpoint. The guards approached, and the driver rolled the window down so that they could see the ambassador in the back. He waved to them, and the limo drove onto the grounds. The driver pulled up before the front door, and the bodyguards exited. The ambassador's door was opened first, then mine.

The ambassador smiled at me as I got out. "Well, we made it in one piece, safe and sound."

As we walked inside the building, I said, "Remember. Make sure that we meet with the president alone. No one else in the room—no advisors, no one."

Robert said, "Don't worry. I have a direct line to him, and I'll make that point very clear and specific when they arrive here. Remember, friendship is an irresistible lady that we can never say 'no' to."

I nodded. "That's a new expression to me. I like it. You're right—when we have faith and friendship with someone, it's hard to say no to that person, even when we aren't very happy at saying yes."

We walked through the residence past the security guards who were spread out in a clear pattern to maintain vigilance. Zuyen greeted us as our escort entered, and she smiled broadly at the pair of us.

She said, "Well, well—I don't think you guys need an introduction anymore. You look like a couple of old friends coming back from a party where you had a great time."

A distinguished-looking butler in his early fifties, tall and dark-skinned with some grey at his temples, greeted us. "Dinner is ready, Mr. Ambassador," he said to Robert.

"Thank you, Thomas," Robert replied.

"Follow me, please," said Thomas as he led the way into the dining room. "This dinner is made with a great deal of love. Zuyen did not let anyone touch any dish. She did everything herself, and the chef is a little jealous. She did not even let him prepare the salad." He took our coats and winked at me.

We sat down at the large dining table. Robert asked Zuyen jokingly, "What is the special occasion that we're celebrating? Or is all this food simply because Dr. Valentine hasn't eaten all day?"

She said, "The special occasion is that Dr. Valentine is alive and managed to bring me home to you today in one piece. I'm really in debt to him for that. He is our guest of honor. You might give him the room we bestow upon our guests of honor and make certain that he is comfortable."

The ambassador smiled as he glanced at me. "Yes, we already discussed that, and he has agreed to stay with us."

"Good!" she exclaimed, her eyes brightening. "That is the least we can do for him."

Thomas asked me, "Do you prefer champagne or wine, sir?"

"Either one is fine. I don't drink very much alcohol, but on occasions like this, among good friends, I usually drink either. If I really trust the people I'm around, sometimes I take a little Grand Marnier as a cordial for dessert."

The ambassador smiled at that. I held up my empty champagne glass. I continued, "In my line of work, I cannot drink this very much. Especially given what a lightweight I am. A little bit makes my legs feel like they're made of rubber bands. The one thing I could never afford to lose is my legs. I could not run from my enemies, and that would make me easy prey."

Everyone, including Thomas, smiled at my jest. Robert said, "If you have no objection, let's start with champagne. We should celebrate our first dinner that we get to have with Dr. Valentine. As we have our delicious appetizers, Zuyen, why don't you tell us of your incredible adventure in the taxi today?"

Zuyen began to relate the story, and Thomas left to begin serving the main course. Zuyen and I made occasional eye contact and smiled. We raised our glasses together and I said, "*Salud, amor, y pesetas.* As they say in Spain, health, love, and money, and time to enjoy them."

Robert said, "For a long, healthy, trustworthy, and loyal relationship."

Zuyen added, "To love, loyalty, and the taxi driver, José, because he brought us together on this beautiful night. And to a great friend, Dr. Valentine."

I smiled in embarrassment and nodded my acknowledgement. "Thank you, but I'm the one who has to be thankful, for meeting you. Even though this was my original destination, it never crossed my mind in my wildest dreams that I would meet such exquisite persons like you and Robert today."

We shared in the smile and sipped our champagne. Time passed as we ate that wonderful meal—and drank nearly two bottles of champagne. We enjoyed the conversation immensely.

Zuyen said, "You won't believe me, but I had never taken a taxi before today."

"Really?" I asked. "Why not?"

She looked guiltily at her father. She indicated him with her glass. "Because my father had always told me not to use a taxi. He prohibited me from using public transportation. He's told me thousands of—"

Robert interrupted, "*Millions.*"

She smiled. "Millions of times not to do it, for security reasons. He gave me such a hard time when I called him to tell him what had happened today. I know I could have told him a different story, but I cannot lie to my father. I love him too much. And I'm glad I didn't, because I would have been caught in the lie just now. As the Bible says, the truth will set you free."

She gave me a smile I thought very cute. "That is why we can speak so freely just now." She shook her head slightly. "As I explained to him, my car wouldn't start in the parking lot of the mall, and so for whatever reason, I didn't listen to the advice he gave me thousands—"

"*Millions*," Robert again interjected.

"OK, Dad, *millions* of times, to call the limo. I was in an adventurous and dangerous mood today. I just walked into the street, and poof! There was a taxi, right in front of me, so I just jumped in. Boy, was I scared when I saw you on the floor of that cab! It crossed my mind at once that Dad was right. Here I was, confronted with a terrorist, and he was going to cut my throat or cut off my head. That's what they do to prisoners, and they send the heads to the families. I thought this is what I deserved for not listening to my father."

She looked at him and gave him an exaggerated pout. "Even though nothing bad happened, and I'm glad it all turned out well, but that was the first and last taxi I will ever take in my life."

Robert grinned from ear to ear. He shook his head. "You don't have to say that twice. I know now you've learned your lesson. I've always wondered why people won't learn simply from the advice of others."

Zuyen shook her head and smiled. "Because, until you experience the pain yourself, like the scare Dr. Valentine gave me, you don't get the lesson you remember for the rest of your life."

I smiled. "I'm sorry. That was the last thing in my mind. It wasn't my intention to scare you so badly. You were just in the wrong place at the wrong time."

"Exactly!" the ambassador exclaimed triumphantly. "That is what I've been trying to spare her from."

"Don't worry," Zuyen assured me. "My father will be in debt to you for life, because I get now what he's been telling me every day but I refused to listen to."

Robert wiped his mouth with his napkin. Still beaming, he said, "You don't have to apologize. You really have done the greatest favor to my angel. I've told her millions of times that I would rather see her walk home if she has car trouble than to take any kind of public transit. In my ambassadorial position, anyone might want to kidnap her just to make a point."

"Yes," I agreed. "You're 100% correct. But, unfortunately, until we experience for ourselves, we don't learn the lessons of life."

Robert said, "My daughter is an angel, but like her mother, she's a rebellious one. Once in a while, she'll do crazy things like this."

Zuyen nodded. "OK, Papa. No more reprimands in front of Dr. Valentine, please. I got it. He gave me a really good reason to never set foot in a taxi, ever again. But you already reprimanded me today enough for the whole year ahead of us." She smiled broadly as she spoke.

"OK, OK," Robert said. He held his glass up to Thomas for a refill. His glass still held aloft, he said, "Who can fight with that smile?"

We all grinned at that. Robert looked at his watch. "Oh, my God! It's three a.m.!"

"What?" I exclaimed. "My God, it's true what they say in Cuba. When you're having fun, time not only flies—it evaporates!"

Zuyen said, "Don't worry about me. I'm a night person and function better this late. I prefer to sleep until noon." She smiled guiltily.

Robert stood up. "While this meal has been great, I need to go to sleep. I have to be up early in the morning."

I said, "Thank you very much for everything. I really appreciate your hospitality and your help."

"You are very welcome, Dr. Valentine," he replied. "It's a pleasure to help you. We'll see each other in the morning—which will come in a very short while."

We all stood up, and Zuyen said to Thomas, "Don't worry about it. Go with my father, and I will show Dr. Valentine to his room."

Thomas bowed as he leaned in to refill my glass. I stopped him with my hand and shake of my head. Zuyen and I left so that she could show me to my quarters. "By the way, Zuyen, Robert already knows my real name. It is Julio Antonio del Mármol. But please keep calling me Dr. Valentine in the meantime for security purposes."

"Can I call you J. Anthony in private? I love that name."

"Yes," I said. "When there's no one else around, that's fine."

We continued walking to a long staircase, nearly touching like a pair of young lovers. When we reached my room, she said, "This is your room for as long as you want to stay."

"Thank you for everything. You're very kind and very sweet. I think I could look at you every night all evening long and never get tired."

She touched my beard and leaned in. We shared a long kiss. She backed away, still holding my hand. "There will be plenty of time for you to look at me later."

"Do you think so?" I murmured with a smile, still close to her. I looked into her beautiful eyes, a blend of the best of European and Asian features. I leaned in to kiss her once more, but she gave me a quick peck on my lips.

"Good night," she said. I watched her as she walked down the corridor. At the corner, she turned back to me and blew me a kiss. She mouthed another good night, and disappeared around the corner.

Eight o'clock the next morning, someone knocked on my door. I heard Zuyen's sweet voice politely saying, "Dr. Valentine, do you mind if I come in? Are you awake?"

I was sitting at a table, writing down some notes. I had only my pants on and a V-neck sleeveless undershirt. My briefcase was on the floor next to me. I covered up the pictures and papers I had scattered on the table. I called out, "Sure, come in. I've been awake for a while."

She came in, wearing a big smile. She carried a tray with orange juice and an assortment of fruit. "Oh, my God! You went to bed so late, and you're up so early! I thought I would find you still in bed."

"No matter how much I wanted to sleep in this morning, my mind wouldn't let me. I have a very busy day ahead of me."

She said, "I know, I know. My father told me a little bit about it. He told me the president of Mexico would be here at noon for lunch, and he told me to let you know to be prepared."

I smiled. "Oh, that is great! I will go and touch up my beard and take a quick shower so that I can appear decently before they come in."

Zuyen put the tray down on the table. "Well, lunch is not going to be until twelve." She smirked at me. "We have about three hours to talk and get to know each other a little better, if you don't mind neglecting your work for a little while."

I understood her suggestion. I took her by the waist and pulled her in close. She put her hand on my partially bared chest. We looked into each other's eyes for a few seconds, and then kissed passionately. She stepped back a little. She went over to the door and locked it. She came back, and we kissed again. We walked over to the sofa. She put her hands behind my neck and began to caress me at the hairline. She pulled her hands away to remove her blouse. She opened her bra, and I saw that the nipples on her peach-colored breasts were hard with excitement. She was breathing heavily, and I grew anxious to see her naked.

I unzipped the side zipper on her skirt and let it fall to the floor. She wore only a G-string with ribbons along the side. I undid my belt and allowed my pants to slowly slide down to the floor. I removed my underwear and pulled her onto the sofa with me. I began to kiss her breasts, slowly moving my way down to her belly, and then lower. She placed both her hands on my head and began to moan in pleasure.

Lightning flashed outside the window, followed by a crash of thunder and the roar of rain coming down hard. As I looked at that display, it seemed as though my body traveled back in time. We made love until we exhausted ourselves, falling asleep in each other's arms. As we slept, I had a strange dream, as if I were connected to my ancestor of the previous century.

I saw a small blonde girl with blue eyes playing with a large, air-filled ball. I took it from her and dropped it overboard from the ship as we came across the ocean from Spain. She began to cry. I had done this to save the life of a slave who had fallen overboard and was drowning. A Spanish naval ship had approached, and the captain was forced to throw several slaves overboard to avoid getting caught with contraband.

I recovered the ball and yelled, "Maria! Maria! It's OK, I've got your ball!" She left off her crying and smiled at me as the slave, now safe, gratefully returned the ball to me. I felt the hands of someone pushing me.

"Dr. Valentine! Dr. Valentine! Are you OK? Are you having a nightmare? Love, are you OK?"

I opened my eyes and saw Zuyen looking at me with wide eyes. She smiled when she saw me open my eyes, and asked, "Who is Maria?"

"What?" I asked in perplexity. "What? What are you saying?"

"Maria. You called to her in your sleep."

I smiled. "Don't worry. She is a little cousin of one of my ancestors, not an old love."

Zuyen smiled. "Are you sure she's not an old love?"

"No, no—one of my ancestors, probably my fourth or fifth cousin. I fell asleep after we made such beautiful love. That is a good sign."

"Yes?" she asked. "Why is that such a good sign?"

"If I fall asleep after making love to you, that means you relaxed my spirit. You are actually in my soul and brought me to my ancestors."

We both smiled and looked deeply into each other's eyes. She said, "You'd better hurry up. You said you need to take a shower, and you only have twenty-five minutes. We both fell asleep."

"Oh, my God!" I exclaimed as I jumped off the sofa.

She said goodbye, gave me a quick kiss, and quietly left the room.

The Communist Reds

The Godless lawyers that only feel jealousy and envy towards others accompanied by hypocrisy are the best individuals who comprise good material to embrace the Reds. Sometimes you can sit and try to understand what is going on in these people's brains. No matter how hard you try to explain it, you have to come to the conclusion that you cannot teach a dog to meow or a cat to bark. This is simply not in their nature. They will not change; they will die like that. The only thing to do is to pray to God that one day they will wake up or wish with all your heart that they go far away so that they don't harm anyone.

Dr. Julio Antonio del Mármol

Chapter 7

THE PRESIDENTIAL WARNING

I showered, dressed hurriedly, and as I was about to open the door to leave, it was opened by Thomas, who had come to escort me. I followed him to the beautiful garden of the embassy, next to the pool. There were beautiful tables with baskets of fruit and a great deal of security surrounding us. The president of Mexico was already there, sitting at a table with the ambassador.

I approached the table and Robert introduced me. The President said, "I have to admit that I was very impressed when my friend Robert told me that you did not work for anyone, that you didn't receive a paycheck from anyone. I told myself this is an extraordinary man that I have to meet. That is very unusual these days. No one does anything unless he's paid for it. Even when you pay for it, things don't always get done properly."

I smiled as I sat down. "Thank you, Mr. President. I do this because I have a debt of gratitude to every democracy in the world. Since you are trying to establish here in your country a free democracy, I wanted to place myself at your disposal and offer my personal friendship to you, not only as the president of this country but as an individual."

He handed me a card with a telephone number. "This is my private number. If you ever need anything in this country, feel free to call."

"Thank you for your confidence," I replied. "Let's hope I never have to use this to bother you."

He shook his head. "It won't be a bother at all. It will be a pleasure to hear from you, especially after what you've done for my family and me."

I replied, "I see Robert has already debriefed you. As I told him, you don't have to worry about it. I do this with the greatest pleasure."

He and I both stood up and shook hands. His security came over to us, and we walked through the garden. I pulled out of my pocket a copy of the cassette with the conversation with the taxi driver. I handed it to him. "This man is the link to yesterday's success at the airport."

The president put his hand on my shoulder. "Fine. I understand. I will meet with you here tonight at eight o'clock. I will bring two of my most trusted advisers. They are in charge of the security of my family. Even if we don't discuss everything in front of them, I want you to meet them. I'd like you to give me your best reading of them, so that I know whether I've placed their safety in good hands or not."

"It will be my pleasure," I said with a nod. I pressed my lips together in conviction.

We shook hands and embraced. We said our goodbyes as Zuyen and Robert joined us to add theirs as well. The president walked across the patio as I walked with Robert to his office to make a phone call. Zuyen followed us.

The phone on the other end rang. When it was answered, I said, "José?"

"Yes?"

"José Angel Gonzalez Martinez?"

"Yes," José said.

"Do you remember me? We talked yesterday."

"Yes, Doctor, I remember you very clearly. I slept with your face in my head."

"Thank you for keeping me in mind, José. I want you to meet me at this address at eight o'clock tonight. I want you to meet my friends and corroborate the details we discussed yesterday." I gave him the address for the embassy, which he repeated in confirmation.

"Don't worry, Dr. Valentine, I'll be there at eight o'clock," he said. We said goodbye and hung up. Robert looked at me with curiosity in his eyes and an unconvinced expression on his face.

"Do you think he will come?" he asked dubiously.

I stroked my chin. "Absolutely, he will be here."

Zuyen smiled in agreement. "Of course he'll be here. Dr. Valentine has a great power to convince people to do as he asks them."

She pointed at my umbrella, which sat in a special pocket in my briefcase. "He has great friends to help him." She asked me in a sarcastic tone, "Have you introduced my father to your friend, Dr. Valentine?"

"No," I said. "I have not had a chance to share with him such intimate details."

Robert noticed our smiles and glances, and felt a little out of the loop. "I only know what you've told me," he said. "I have no idea how these things function."

I picked up my umbrella and showed Robert how the knife and gun functioned. Robert was fascinated. "Oh, I want one like this! This would be a good associate and friend to have in a dangerous situation."

"Yes, my friend," I replied. "She could be your best companion. I designed it, and a good friend in Italy made it for me. He first made it with only a single shot, but I told him I needed the capacity to fire two or three bullets. He remade it to my specification. This is the prototype, and I was thinking to patent it for mass marketing one day. However, I've found it so valuable that I don't want any competition."

"Would you mind, if you ever make others, to make one for me?" Robert asked. "You know that one would be never used against you."

"Well," I said, "perhaps—as long as someone doesn't steal it from you and I find someone shooting at me in the airport with my own toy."

We all smiled. Robert said, "Well, it's been a great pleasure to see you, but I have to go to the embassy."

"I have to go into the city, as well," I said.

Zuyen said with a smile, "I can take you to the city, if you would like."

"Oh, it would be a great pleasure to go with you," I said.

We said goodbye to the ambassador and parted ways. Zuyen approached the security desk where a very thin, dark man sat on duty.

The guard said, "Your car has been fixed and is waiting for you in the garage."

"What was wrong with it, Damian?" Zuyen asked. "What did you find out?"

"It was a simple problem with the battery. They replaced it with a new one."

"Thank you very much," Zuyen replied.

"No problem, Miss Zuyen. It's always a pleasure." His answer didn't sound sincere to me. He sounded as if he were hiding the truth from her. Although my training had taught me to read the demeanor and physical expressions of people to know if they're lying or not, I thought it was possible I might be getting paranoid.

I looked at her as we walked through the garden, admiring her figure. She turned and smiled at me. "Is something wrong?"

I didn't want to scare her with my suspicions, so I replied, "I was just admiring your beauty."

She looked down in embarrassment. "You probably say that to everyone. With all of your experience in traveling around the world, you probably say that to every woman you meet. Like a sailor, you probably have a woman in every port in the world."

I clapped my hands to my breast. "Oh! That hurt!"

"Is it not true?" she asked.

"No, it isn't. Why do you women always assume that all men are the same breed of dog with the same fleas? You do not realize how very different we are, but you will get it very soon. I'm about to leave for the Caribbean islands. Why don't you come with me so that you can get to know me a little better? I have a nice place on St. Martin Island. You might enjoy the atmosphere there. At the same time, you will get to know me a lot better."

She smiled. "Really? You want me to go with you? Wouldn't I interfere with your dangerous business? I've never been to St. Martin's."

I replied, "It's the most beautiful island in the entire Caribbean—after Cuba, of course. It's half French, half Dutch. You will be fascinated, since you love shopping. You'll have the best of both worlds there."

She smiled slyly and came over to me. She put her hands between mine and said, "Really? You want to get to know me a little better?"

I kissed her hands. "Yes. From the moment I met you in the taxi. You entered like a beautiful butterfly into my heart. I looked at you and you made me happy. I don't know if this is love, but I haven't felt this way in a long, long time. Even then, it's never felt this strong." I gave her a soft, tender kiss, and we walked from the residence to the garage.

Zuyen hit the garage door button to open it. We walked over to a mint green Jaguar convertible. She tied her hair behind her as we got in. She picked up a visor and put it on. She was wearing an expensive jogging suit with matching white shoes. The suit had a triple stripe pattern running down the side.

As she got into the car, I looked at her. She said, "What? You keep looking at me like that."

"Nothing," I replied. "I just like the way you look."

She smiled, thanked me, and started the car. We drove out of the garage. I asked if I could use her car phone. She nodded and handed it to me. I dialed a number. When it was answered, I said, "General, this is Dr. Valentine. Are you available?"

"Yes, I've been waiting for your call, Dr. Valentine."

"I'm on my way right now. The same place as usual."

"OK," he said. "I'll be there in fifteen to twenty minutes."

I hung up and gave Zuyen instructions as to our destination. We arrived a few minutes later at the shopping mall. A dark sedan was waiting for us.

Zuyen asked, "How much time do you need?"

I checked my watch. "Give me a couple of hours. Go do your things. If you're a little late, don't worry about it. I will be waiting for you at this spot."

We both smiled and exchanged a quick kiss. I exited the car and approached the sedan. There were three men in the car—the driver and two passengers. One was in his fifties with white hair at his temples. The man in the passenger seat opened the door for me.

"Dr. Valentine," he said, "the general is waiting for you."

I got into the car and greeted the Mexican general. He was a small man with a receding hairline.

"Hello," he replied. "It's nice to see you alive and healthy. What have you been eating these days? You look younger each time I see you. What is your secret?"

"My secret is a constant adrenaline rush," I said. We both laughed.

"Join the club," he replied with a smirk.

I added, "It also helps to eat a lot of chicken, fish with no oil, and to avoid chili picante."

The general clapped his hand to his forehead. "Uh-oh! If I cannot have chili, I would rather die. That is my passion. For me, chili habanero is like sex: the hotter the picante is, the better— even if it makes me cry. I love my chili picante *bien picosos*[20]."

I shook my head. "I'll tell you something, my friend. What I brought you today might make you cry without those chili *picosos* in your mouth."

I leaned back in my seat and removed the tape recorder from the briefcase. "This is the complete plan to assassinate your president. Is that hot enough to make you cry? They not only want to destabilize Mexico, but the entire region. They want to close the border to the United States and cause tremendous chaos through

---

[20] Very, very hot

all South and Central America so that they can create a conflict between the United States and Mexico. Then they will sit down and enjoy that conflict."

The smile dropped off the general's face and he grew grim. He squeezed his bottom lip. "Huh. That extreme, eh? That is the way these people are playing the game now?"

I adjusted my sunglasses. "Why are you surprised? They have been playing this game for over forty years. If not Chile, then it's El Salvador, Panama, Bolivia, Honduras, Colombia, Venezuela, and now Mexico. They're trying to destroy the whole political system and destabilize the democracies around the entire world. You know their game, General. They take our youth from the universities and colleges and offer them free scholarships. Then they brainwash them and send them back to their countries or other countries to die for the Marxist proletariat cause. You've actually been one of the lucky ones, since you've been considered a friendly country to them. If they treat you like this, imagine what it's like for their enemies!"

The general shook his head and said sadly, "I don't want to know. This is unbelievable. They're going too far this time!" He put the earpiece from the player into his ear, and I played it for him. I looked through my briefcase and pulled out a folder. I removed several pictures of two men and one woman. They had extremely short black hair, and the woman's had a streak of white. As the general listened to the tape, his facial expression changed from uncomfortable to irritated. His face flushed as he shook his head.

Our car reached the city limits, and the general signaled to the driver to pull over. He got out, and the bodyguard followed. With a worried expression on his face, he walked into the forest. I followed and handed him the pictures.

"These are the three individuals in charge of executing the targets," I explained. "They are called *Sueño Negro*—the Black Dream."

"They are already in place?"

"From what I understand, they left Cuba yesterday. They should be in Mexico by now."

The general crossed himself. "My God! What happened to the traditional way to fight? Why kill people this way?"

"Because this way, nobody has any suspicions of an assassination. It won't create any problems, and it gives them the time to do what they want to do."

The general shook his head once more in disgust. He put his face in both hands and looked up. "Aaah," he said in exasperation. "Well, we have to say one thing: they are very sophisticated. They are good at what they do, and they're getting better every day. Now they're using biological weapons. We have very little time to stop this."

"My friend," I said, "I have a major, major problem on my hands on the other side of the border. It's going to be much bigger than this. But that's why I'm sticking around here. We *have* to stop this first."

The general nodded.

"Let me explain how this is supposed to work," I said. "They'll introduce this substance through toothpaste—all they need is a few drops. It's a toxic substance that enters the brain and only kills the cells that signal when the body needs rest. The victim can no longer go to sleep—like having chronic insomnia. That is why it is called Black Dream. The worst part is that the substance is untraceable; after it does the damage, it dissolves completely. This particular enzyme makes the person feel so good, like he's constantly high on cocaine. The body accepts it like a caffeine pill. It stimulates the brain so much that the person no longer cares that they're not sleeping. He can function twenty-four hours a day and needs to eat very little. When he starts to experience natural fatigue but cannot fall asleep, he may go to a doctor. The doctor will not find anything wrong. Eventually, he reaches the point of total exhaustion, and he drops dead from it. The death certificate will read 'natural causes,' because no test will reveal any foreign substance."

The general shook his head and put his arm around my shoulder. "My friend, we're not fighting a normal enemy. We're fighting the devil himself. These people are so unscrupulous and cunning in their craft that they've given me goosebumps." He rubbed his arms.

"General, remember, the devil is older, and this guy's been at it for forty years. He has the entire country at his disposal—scientists with no ethics experimenting on prisoners on that island. They've been playing this game for so long and have such resources they have surpassed whatever the human mind could imagine. All we can do is try to stop them. It's a daily race; while they build castles on the sand, and we have to rush to bring them down. My only question is what to do when we can no longer stop it."

The general had an expression of extreme worry. He looked at me and said, "I think this time they've gone too far. My question is who has been supplying these people with all these sophisticated chemicals for them to develop this kind of weapon?"

I replied, "Russia, China, even some with no scruples within the U.S. government. Remember, we have all these weapons. It just happens that their mad scientists have been working for them for so long, they've caught up with us. Now the genie is out of the bottle. The major problem is that there's no cure for this condition after the substance has been introduced into the body. Our investigation has revealed that it is derived from a small Brazilian fruit that grows in the Amazon. The natives used to eat the fruit for energy, but the adverse reaction was that the energy could be prolonged for a few months before the person died. It doesn't hurt the organs but maintains the brain at complete performance. A small drop is all that is needed to terminate the life of someone in a matter of months, no matter how physically fit and strong that person is."

The general asked with concern, "You told me the president already has knowledge about these plans?"

"Yes. He has not only the knowledge but the pictures, too. I left you copies of those photos and documents. The only thing I cannot leave in your possession is the cassette. I cannot jeopardize the people in Cuba who got the information to me."

"I understand," the general said in a convinced tone. He raised his right arm and put it on my shoulder. "I'm going to take all the precautions I can and call the people in charge of the president's security so that we can stay alert and take action. All I have to say is, thank you very much, Dr. Valentine. We will never be able to repay you for this invaluable work for our country and our freedom."

"Don't worry about it," I said. "I do it with real pleasure."

We walked back to the car. As we walked, the general said, "I'm actually really proud of you. You are a man without a country or a flag, but you embrace every country and flag in order to defend them. That makes you an international hero."

I smiled. "I don't know about that. But I can tell you that I have more than one mother that I've sworn to protect, and one of them is Mexico."

The general smiled at me and nodded. In a voice thick with emotion, he said, "My friend, when we're done with this craziness, I want to invite you to my house in Cancun so you can meet my family. I want to have the honor of offering you a roasted pig with black beans and fried mashed bananas so that I can see the satisfaction in your face."

I smiled again. "General, you know how to hit a man in his heart with joy. It will be an honor for me to meet your family."

We got in the car, and the driver took us back to the mall where we had initially met. Once there, he parked underground, and we both got out. We shook hands, embraced, and said our goodbyes. I looked around casually and saw Zuyen's car. She was standing outside it, waiting for me. I walked towards her, and she hurried to meet me. When she got to me, she gave me a hug.

"You guys took longer than I expected. I've been waiting for a while, and I started to worry. So many scenarios went through my mind."

When we got into the car, she asked, "Where are we going?"

I took a slip of paper out of my pocket and handed it to her. "To this address, please."

She took the note and read it before starting the engine. "OK," she said with a nod.

As we drove out of the underground garage, I picked up her car phone once more and dialed a number. After a few rings, a voice answered the phone, "José Angel Gonzalez Martinez, at your service."

I smiled. "Yes, José. It's me, Dr. Valentine."

"Oh! How are you doing? It's great to hear from you!"

I replied, "Is there any way you can arrive early to the address I gave you this morning, please?"

"How early?" he asked.

"Perhaps an hour earlier than I mentioned."

"No problem. You can count on me. I'll be there at seven o'clock."

"Thank you," I answered. "That is perfect." I hung up.

Zuyen was looking at me in puzzlement. "Do you have any doubts that he will show up to the meeting?"

I stroked my chin and shook my head. "Well, I don't want to take any chances."

We pulled up in a very poor neighborhood. Zuyen had to drive carefully to avoid the children playing baseball in the street. She stopped outside the house at the address I had given her. We got out and walked up to the door. I knocked.

A short, fat woman answered the door, holding it partially closed defensively. She said, "*Buenos dias.* How can I help you?"

I asked, "Is this the house of José Angel Gonzales Martinez?"

She looked surprised. "Yes. Who wants to know?"

The screams of the children playing got louder, and the ball bounced up next to us. One of the children ran up next to me to retrieve it. "Excuse me, sir," he said. I moved my feet out of his way and smiled at him.

I replied to the lady, "I am Dr. Valentine. Are you José's wife?"

She smiled. "Yes."

I pulled an envelope out of my pocket and handed it to her. "Would you please give this to José? Tell him that Dr. Valentine left this little gift and a small tip to buy some toys for the children." She nervously smiled as she hesitatingly took the envelope. It wasn't completely sealed, and her eyes brightened as she saw the number of $100 bills inside it. She smiled broadly and opened the door fully. "Oh, thank you! I am Maria Isabel. Would you like to come in and have some tea or coffee or something? God bless you!"

I smiled again. "No, thank you. I have to go. But say hello to José for me."

Zuyen had been standing next to me. She tilted her head down so she could look at Maria over the rims of her sunglasses, and smiled at her.

"God bless you both, Dr. Valentine!" Maria said.

We smiled and waved modestly as we turned and left. When we got back into the car, Zuyen asked with a mischievous smile, "Where to next?"

"Home," I said. "We'll have the meeting in a few hours."

"I'm not going to ask you what I want to know. But to satisfy my curiosity a little bit, please tell me how you got that address. You don't have to answer or tell me anything that could compromise you. I know for a fact, though, that when you told her to say hello to José from you, something was cooking in your brain. You are extremely smart."

Still smiling, I answered, "Thank you. It's part of my job. If you're not smart, you don't survive. I think you're smart, too, to be able to catch on to what I'm doing. Some people don't get it so quickly."

We entered the back of the house on the embassy grounds. Before we entered the garage, her car phone rang. Zuyen answered, "Hello?"

José's voice answered. "Dr. Valentine?"

Zuyen said, "Hold on, please." She handed me the phone.

"Hello?" I said.

José said, "Thank you very much for the gift. You didn't have to bother yourself with that."

"No bother at all," I replied. "It's a symbolic gesture of appreciation for your family and all your troubles."

José replied, "No, no, sir—it's no trouble at all. I do it with great satisfaction. I will be there ten or fifteen minutes ahead of time."

I smiled. "Thank you, José." We said goodbye and hung up.

Zuyen was smiling again. She drove into the garage as the automatic door opened. She parked, and we got out and walked into the house. The servants helped her with her bags as I tried to help with some of the smaller packages. A servant rushed to take them from me.

I said to Zuyen, "I'm going to my room to refresh myself and maybe change my clothes. I've been thinking of that bathtub all afternoon, so maybe I'll take a long bath."

She winked at me. She leaned in and whispered, "I would love to rub your back, but I have to go to my father and unpack my stuff. Maybe later, this time together?"

I murmured, "In that case, I'll just freshen up and save the bath for later. It will make the thought much more appealing to anticipate."

A few hours later, I walked through the hallway, now dressed in one of my finest suits—white, with my family crest monogramed on the right breast—and a navy blue T-shirt underneath. I walked up to a set of double doors where two Marines stood, one on either side. Additionally, two men in black suits and ties walked around in the corridor, their eyes constantly scanning the area. José was seated outside near the bodyguards.

José smiled when he saw me. "I already did what you told me to do. I'll stick around a little longer in case you need me."

"Thank you, José," I said.

Chapter 8

A DECOY FOR A SOLUTION

The Marines admitted me, and inside, seated at a long table, were the president of Mexico and the United States ambassador. Two other men sat at the table with them.

I looked at both my watches and said, "Now I feel bad. I thought I was going to be punctual, and now it looks like I'm late."

"No," Robert said, "we're early. Even your guy outside, José, was early. Since we were early, we've been talking here. There's no question in the president's mind that this is an extremely delicate situation, and the danger is very clear. His question is how to solve this problem without revealing the identity of who provided the information to you."

The president rubbed his eyebrows. "You have to understand, Dr. Valentine, we cannot accuse a foreign country without tangible proof. At least, not publicly. What do you think, Armando?"

The other man, Armando, raised his left hand and nodded. "Yes, Mr. President, this is a very delicate situation we have on our hands. But we have to think about first things first. We have to address your security as the top priority, and then we can address everything else. According to the taxi driver, this is neither the first nor the last assassination they will plan from the Cuban embassy. We know for a fact that these Cuban communists are not only conniving and vindictive, but they are also extremely dangerous and highly sophisticated."

The president tossed the pictures of the two men and the woman onto the table. "All these individuals hold high positions in our government. The woman is one of the people I trust the most. She is around my family, for God's sake! How can we arrest these people and expose the truth if we don't have any facts to convict them, much less to execute an arrest?"

His expression was one of frustration and impotent anger. He looked at the other man, an older man with graying hair and a thick Pancho Villa mustache, wearing thick reading glasses. "Javier, what is your assessment?"

Javier leaned back. He could not conceal his worry and conflicted feelings. "Mr. President, I agree one hundred percent with Armando. This is not only extremely delicate, but it's very complex. We have to take into consideration that the Cuban embassy and their government will deny absolutely everything, feign offense, and demand an explanation should we level any accusations against them."

Javier snatched the photos and stared hard at them. He shook his head. "I hate to tell you this, Mr. President, but in my experience, the best approach is to physically eliminate everyone involved in this without bringing any charges or making it public. We don't have to tell anyone outside this room. The only way to resolve the problem without serious complications is to kill the dog in order to cure the rabies. Is that not an old saying in your country, Dr. Valentine?"

I smiled slightly while everyone else lapsed into silence.

Javier tossed the pictures onto the table, removed his glasses, and dropped them on top of the photos. He continued, "The question is, who and what department in our government can be trusted to discretely take on this mission in complete silence? We don't have any room for improvisation. This could complicate the situation even further."

All eyes turned to Robert, waiting for his comment. I had been taking stenographic notes in a small book while everyone else spoke. The president had a worried expression. As he stroked his chin, he looked at everyone in the room. His eyes flicked to me in puzzlement several times.

He stroked his mustache and said, "You're writing notes in that little book, my friend. You've got my curiosity running at a thousand miles per hour. Have you been brainstorming?"

"Something like that, Mr. President. I've been taking notes on what everyone says and noting everyone's opinions. This is important, because the opinions of all the intelligent men in this room could come together to form a brilliant plan to solve the problem. Things like this require everyone to get involved."

All of them looked at me in wonder with the exception of Robert, who smiled, clearly expecting an answer along the lines of the one I had given. The president replied, "Please, be completely open, Dr. Valentine, if you have any suggestions. You've been very quiet. My question is, if you were the one with this problem, how would you handle it?"

I leaned back in my seat and flipped back a few pages in my notebook. "I agree with Javier one hundred percent—the first step is to eliminate the threat to you and your family. You don't know how extensive their plans are. We don't know what else they may be planning to do. Physical elimination of this first team won't tell us whether or not there's a second or third team already in motion in case they are intercepted. I'm going to put myself at your service. I have professionals who are discreet, but I can have no interference from the government. All I need is a green light from you in case the situation doesn't go exactly according to plan. No one will be able to associate it with your government. I'm talking about professionals with twenty or thirty years of experience. Nobody, without exception, will know what we are going to do. This is not negotiable."

Robert looked at me intensely. He reached out and put his right hand on my shoulder. He said to the president, "My friend, I believe strongly that if anyone can do this for you, Dr. Valentine can."

I smiled. "I sort of agree with Armando that the level of sophistication of these assassins is, it is safe to say, the level of a PhD in crime. I don't say this just from past experience but also from the recent attempt on my life that took place in the airport. I think my response to them must have been shocking and sent a strong message back to our enemies that they're not going to be dealing with amateurs here in Mexico. They know we're professionals, and if we do this properly, they'll get the message to leave their filthy hands out of the internal affairs of Mexico."

Robert looked worried. "Yes, but how can we expose this to the public without revealing your contact? We have to have a valid reason."

The president nodded emphatically. "Do you have any suggestions, Dr. Valentine?"

Without hesitation, I said, "Yes, I do."

The president asked, "Would you please explain what you have in mind?"

I scratched at my hairline. "Do you remember during Reagan's administration, in the '80s, the Iran-Contra affair?"

The president smiled. "Yes, I do. He was the president of the United States that I most admired."

I smiled. "Well, Iran-Contra was only a decoy to distract public attention away from the Zipper, which was a much larger operation. At that time, it was the largest ever for the United States, and probably will be for many years to come. To this day, nobody ever really knew that the Zipper existed."

The president removed his Stetson and put it on the table, his curiosity ready to explode. Everyone else in the room's attention was riveted on me. I took a sip from a glass of water on the table. I continued, "I want you to understand that the Contra affair wasn't created. It was an opportunity which simply happened. The press ran with it. All we did was use it to divert attention away from what we were doing. We just stretched the situation to create a little controversy. The Zipper was the larger plan that we wanted to conceal. It brought down the economy of the entire Soviet bloc in

Europe, and like a mudslide, it brought down the Berlin Wall. No one ever knew that the operation existed."

I looked the president in the eyes. "You understand, sir? You need to find a decoy to use as an excuse to break off relations with Cuba. This way, you send the Cuban government a message. All you need is a small decoy."

I looked at the watch on my left hand and pointed at it. "From now on, the clock is ticking, every second, every minute, every hour. There are several things happening right now in your country. Just pick one to send Cuba that message to keep their hands off Mexico and respect the people's right to live in peace under a democracy. The result will be the same as if we publicly proclaimed the truth."

The president smiled as he stroked his mustache again. "Dr. Valentine, I have to thank you again for risking your life for me, my family, and my country."

"For me, it's a pleasure, Mr. President," I replied. "And I offer to you, as I've offered to Robert, my personal friendship. I'm going to ask you, if you don't mind, to think this over for twenty-four hours."

He looked at Armando and Javier. Javier smiled and said, "I think we already have the perfect decoy, Mr. President: Guadalajara." He raised his eyebrows suggestively. "It's in the early stages, but I think in a few years we'll have something we can use out of that." The president nodded his head and smiled.

"Very well," I replied. "That is very good, a great advantage. I will stay in Mexico for another twenty-four hours and wait for your answer."

Everyone stood up and shook hands with each other. We walked towards the door. José was anxiously waiting for me in the hallway, a big smile on his face. I excused myself from the group and walked over to him. I shook his hand and patted him firmly on the shoulder.

"Thank you," I said to him.

"OK," he said. "If you need anything, call me." He walked outside to where his taxi cab was parked before the front door.

The group walked to the dining room, where the servants were setting the table and bringing in drinks. Zuyen was joining us as well. We all sat down in preparation to eat. Security was very heavy because of the combined presence of the U.S. ambassador and the president of Mexico.

As we sat down, one of the guards rushed in and whispered in the president's ear. His eyes opened wide and he looked at me. I didn't like that look at all. He shook his head. Two more guards entered with grim expressions on their pale faces. The president grimaced and put his hand on his face.

He said, "I'm sorry, Dr. Valentine, but I have to tell you that your friend, the taxi driver, was just killed outside. A long shot from a sniper caught him in the head."

I sprang up, grabbed my briefcase, and headed for the door, but the guards blocked me. I looked at the president, who gestured for them to let me go. I pulled my umbrella out and ran out through the garden to where the taxi cab was.

I pulled a pair of latex gloves out of my briefcase and started to inspect the body. There was a bullet hole in the window, and in his temple. Based on the angle, I was able to look across the street to the building where the shot probably came from. The guards were speaking over their radios, while the guards inside the embassy gardens were running around with dogs. A helicopter started to land on the pad in the embassy patio. I pulled out a pair of small binoculars and scanned the rooftop across from us. I didn't find the sniper or anything suspicious.

I went back to the room where the guards had been holding everyone for their security until the all-clear signal was given. I shook my head and said, "He's dead, and the shooter is gone."

One of the guards said, "Mr. President, we have to leave this area immediately. We have no positive identification of the sniper or any idea of his current location."

The president nodded and walked a few steps over to me. He put his hand on my left shoulder and murmured to me, "You don't need twenty-four hours. You have the green light *now*. If you can do this, we will owe you a great favor. But do it immediately and cleanly."

Javier, Armando, and Robert were all close by and could hear what he said. They exchanged glances and smiled. I looked at him and nodded. I said, "Don't worry about it at all. Everything will be done at the speed of light and it will be done properly." I looked at Armando and Javier and said, "You guys do your part. We will do ours."

We shook hands, and the president left with his guards for the helicopter. We could hear the sirens of the ambulance and local police approaching. I walked out onto the patio, Zuyen following nervously. She was obviously scared. I went inside to use the phone.

"O'Brien," I said when he answered. "I need you right here. As soon as possible, please."

"Is it that important?"

"Absolutely. This could be their first move to destabilize the entire region. I need you here tonight if possible. The blue ribbon just broke. Please advise my team. Call Elizabeth, and tell her we need her as soon as possible here."

"OK. I'll be there tonight. Goodbye."

"Thank you." I hung up. We walked back to the dining room where Robert and his guards were still sitting. I excused myself to make another phone call.

"General?"

"Yes, Dr. Valentine. I've been waiting for your call."

"We have the green light. You will maintain yourself and your men on standby. We will handle the whole thing. You don't have to worry about it at all."

"If that is the way the president wants it, that's fine with me," he said. "Go ahead, be my guest."

I laughed. "Literally. I am, after all, your guest. Thank you very much."

We hung up. Zuyen and Robert were watching me in silence, the expressions on their faces reflecting their anxious worry in the midst of all the excitement. We could see through the garden window the blue and red flashing lights of the police cars. We looked out and saw José's body being loaded into the ambulance while a tow truck prepared to take the taxi away. There was security everywhere. It started to rain.

The guards headed for their shelter to get out of the rain. I was still on the phone, trying to locate some of the people on my team. The major domo, Thomas, asked us if we were going to eat. We had all lost our appetite and replied in the negative.

Robert said, "Though we're not going to eat, bring us some wine, Thomas. That will help us relax after the stress of this night."

I nodded. "That's not a bad idea."

Thomas went and returned moments later with some wine. He poured three glasses. We talked for a little while about what had just happened as we finished the bottle. Then we said good night to each other and retired to our rooms.

About ten minutes later, I started to run the Jacuzzi. I was wearing only my pants when Zuyen knocked on the door. She asked if she could come in, and when I opened the door I saw she was carrying a tray with champagne, cheese, fruit, crackers, and shrimp.

She said, "As I promised, I've come to give you a back rub and take a bath with you to help you relax after this tense evening."

I smiled and we kissed. I took the tray from her hands and we walked towards the bathroom.

A few hours later, we were in bed together, eating what she had brought as we lay under the sheets. The phone rang, and I answered.

"Are you OK?" O'Brien asked.

"Yes. Where are you?"

"I'm in our usual meeting location in this town."

"OK." I checked my watch. It was 4:30 a.m. "I'll be there as soon as possible."

I turned to Zuyen. "I'm sorry, honey, but I have to go and meet my friend."

I picked up the phone. "Operator, please get me the number of the local taxi company."

"Hang up," Zuyen said, "you don't need to do that. Take my car. Or if you need more space for your friends, take the Lincoln Navigator from the garage. It's my father's but he never uses it." She took a key off her keychain and handed it to me. I leaned over to her and gave her a kiss. "Thank you, sweetie. That is going to help."

I dressed quickly and went to the garage as she had directed and took the Lincoln Navigator. I waved to the gate guards and left the embassy to drive into the city. I arrived at the hotel where O'Brien and I normally met and went to the front desk. I was about to show some identification, but the gentleman at the desk recognized me immediately. He handed me a key, and I walked to the elevator. I inserted the key to access the penthouse and went up.

I entered the presidential suite and found O'Brien and Elizabeth waiting for me there, eating French toast and waffles at the table. There was also a fruit basket with fresh cut papaya and a bread basket. We greeted each other.

O'Brien asked, "Do you want something to eat?"

"Yes, as a matter of fact. I didn't have dinner, and I could eat a very large, juicy porterhouse steak right now, like the one I offered you in Long Beach."

"Sorry," he said, "the kitchen is closed. All we could get is this. You can order more, if you like." I sat down and helped myself to the French toast and fruit. O'Brien continued, "Sorry to get you out of bed, but we wanted you to debrief us."

"No problem. I wasn't asleep, I've been waiting for you. Every second that passes, the president and his entire family's life is in jeopardy." I looked at O'Brien seriously. "Did you bring the money to cover our expense, or do I have to print some?"

He looked at me and smiled as he shook his head. He reached inside his coat and pulled out an envelope filled with hundred dollar bills. I opened my briefcase and put the envelope inside. I pulled out two manila envelopes and gave one to each of them. "This is the project. There's no room for any mistake or imprecision. We have to move quickly and cleanly. There can be no evidence, not even bodies. That could complicate the situation even further."

With a piece of French toast on her fork, Elizabeth said jokingly, "Hello, honey, I'm here, too." She blew me a kiss. A freedom fighter who had worked with me since 1971, the redhead was one of my most trusted associates.

"I'm sorry, sweetie," I said. "I haven't eaten today. It's been an extremely stressful day, and this evening didn't finish the way I had planned. They killed my only witness to the entire conspiracy."

"Don't worry at all," she said reassuringly. "I understand. I know you love me anyway." She put her hand underneath the collar of her blouse and made a beating heart with it.

"I'm already done with my breakfast." She smiled and stood up. "We will handle this like a masterpiece."

She took some apples and bananas, saying, "This is for later. I'll leave you guys to discuss the details. I already have your package." She left, closing the door behind her.

While O'Brien ate his waffles, he looked over the file and the photos. He said, "I need you to come back with me tonight. I know this is extremely important, what's going on here, but I've got my hands full back there, as well. The package you sent me resulted in a huge commotion. My people feel like this pill is too big for them to swallow. You know, the same old political stupidities. I need your help to convince the kids that if they eat too much candy they're going to get a stomachache. Then we'll need to give them an Alka-Seltzer."

His tone was rife with marked irony and frustration. He shook his head. "This is not even a shadow of the Old Man that we had as our leader in the 80's."

I examined the folder he brought, and saw the situation was very grim. I took out another envelope and handed him some photos. Then I gave him the cassette recorder and played it after he put the earphones on. "This almost cost me my life the other day."

O'Brien's face slowly grew grimmer. There was even a hint of fear. After he finished, I removed the tape. I took a small plate from the food tray and pulled out a bottle of acid. I put the tape on the plate and poured the acid over it.

"What did you do that for? We should have brought that with us."

"No. No one else needs to hear that. Everyone who needs to has done so already. There's no sense in keeping a time bomb with us. You know I don't like to take unnecessary risks."

He shook his head in disagreement. "Oh, man."

"That's why I called you. You will have to convince them."

He looked uncertain. "Thank you for your confidence in me. But you just destroyed our only evidence. What if I can't?"

I took a piece of waffle and stayed silent for several seconds, smiling at him.

"I don't like it when you smile like that," he said. "What do you have in mind?"

I didn't answer but took a note from my jacket and handed it to him. He looked at it and asked, "What is this?"

"The address of the ambassador's house. Two reasons for that note. First, if you need to verify what you just heard for anyone, who better than the U.S. ambassador? You can use him as a witness for what he heard. The other reason is that we will meet at 7:30 at that address to leave from there. OK?"

We said our goodbyes, and I left the hotel. When I reached the house, the ambassador saw me and commented, "You look like you haven't been able to sleep all night."

"No, I haven't. There's too much to do and too little time."

"Have you had breakfast?"

"Yes, I ate with my friends."

"Oh!" he exclaimed in surprise. "Are they already here?"

"Yes. They're here and ready to go."

He said, "I tried to find Zuyen, but she wasn't there. I assumed she had gone with you."

"Maybe she left early to go jogging or something," I said.

He looked at me skeptically. He hesitated and then said, "I'm going to ask you a favor. Please—don't hurt her. She is the only daughter I have, and I love her very much."

I breathed deeply. "You don't have to worry about it at all. I would rather hurt myself than hurt her, Robert. The same worries you have her security, I have. I don't know if you believe in love at first sight, but I've never before felt the way I feel for your daughter with any other woman. The last thing I have in my mind is to let anything or anyone hurt her. I give you my word of honor that I will do my best to make her happy."

He smiled in satisfaction. I could see he completely accepted my sincerity. He shook his head then and said, "Well, that is a very pleasant thing to know. Now I know I can stop worrying so much. You'll worry for me a little bit." We both smiled. "Zuyen told me that you invited her to your house on St. Martin's."

I looked him in the eyes. "Yes. With my best, most honorable intentions. If you have any objection, I will cancel that invitation, even if I have to break her heart. That is how much I care about your friendship."

"No, no—under no circumstances," he said quickly. "Please, she already asked permission. I told her it was OK with me. You're both adults, and I only asked that you remove her far away from danger. I don't want her to be an innocent casualty in what you're doing."

I smiled. "Precisely. That's why I want to take her to the Caribbean, far away. We'll get to know each other better, and she'll enjoy it very much. If you wish, you can come with us any time. It's fine with me. The invitation is extended to you, as well."

He rushed his answer, "No, no, no. You don't want a chaperone to spoil your secluded, romantic vacation. I'm very grateful for your taking her far away and not involving her in what you're doing. And thank you for your invitation. Next time."

"Very well," I said.

"Since tonight will probably be your last night in Mexico, why don't you invite your friend O'Brien and the rest of your team to eat with us tonight? Since we could not have that dinner with the president, it would be an honor and a delight for me to get to know all your guys at my table. Besides, we will all have a good time."

"OK, sounds like a good idea," I said. "I'll take you up on your invitation. I think you'll be very satisfied with the people I hang around with. 'Tell me who you walk with, and I'll tell you who you are.'"

"It sounds like you're very fond of your friends and your team."

I said with complete conviction, "I can guarantee you with my life that they're good in the same way they would guarantee their lives for me."

"You're very lucky," Robert replied, "and it must be very rewarding to have that caliber of friends around you."

"Yes, indeed."

Robert looked at me with a big smile of admiration. "OK, it's set. Invite them for eight o'clock at my house for dinner, and I'm not taking no for an answer."

I smiled. "I think they'll be delighted. Thank you, Robert. You are a great man."

He grinned and pointed to the umbrella. "I only ask you in exchange to remember that when you breed her, I want a puppy." We both laughed.

Chapter 9

SAVING LIVES

A few hours later, a black van left the Catholic monastery. Inside it were two priests and a nun, riding in silence as they synchronized their watches. One of the priests was a balding man with the vestiges of white hair remaining around the temples. The beautiful young nun watched the cars passing by, her blue eyes catching the headlights of the opposite line of cars. She sat in the passenger's seat while the balding priest drove. The younger priest sat silently in the back seat.

They left the city behind, and drove through the Mexican countryside for a few hours before entering another town. As the early morning sun began to brighten the sky, they drove up to a beautiful residence with an imposing black gate. They stopped at the entry and greeted the soldier on duty. Security was very high and pickets with dogs patrolled the entire grounds. Clearly, something big was expected. The three consecrated religious showed their identification to the sentry.

"Yes, you're here early," he said. "It's six a.m., and you're not supposed to be here until seven or seven-thirty."

The nun replied, "To those who rise early, God provides special help."

The guard smiled and opened the gate. They drove through the beautiful gardens on either side of the long driveway. At the end of the drive a small cottage stood near the main house. Two more secret service agents came out, evidently to give them a double check inspection. They got out of the van.

A woman in her fifties came out of the house and called to the agents, "It's OK, you don't need to check them out. We know them—how many years have they been coming here, for God's sake?" The sentinels stepped back obediently. She walked over and noticed that the faces weren't who she was expecting. "Where is Father Francisco?" she asked the senior priest in surprise. "Who are you?"

The watch dogs, hearing that, slowed their walk back towards the house. The nun jumped in at once. "*Señora* Margarita, *gracia divina*[21], Father Francisco is on a trip to the Vatican. He told me to say hello to you. This is Father Alberto, this is Father Justo, and I am Sister Patricia."

Margarita looked at her suspiciously for a moment, but as she took in Sister Patricia's beautiful face, she softened and smiled. "OK, OK. They didn't tell me they were going to send different people. They've never done that without telling me ahead of time before. Follow me to the house, please." As she showed them the way, she continued, "Our first lady has beautiful taste. Of course, with her perfect figure, who wouldn't? She always tells me to keep some of the clothes for myself if I want to, but I couldn't fit in them even if my life depended on it."

Sister Patricia replied, "Well, Margarita, it's wonderful for you and the first lady to donate all these clothes to charity. That really lightens one's spirit, which is the most important thing for us."

Margarita smiled and nodded. "*Claro, claro.* However, it's not a sin to have both the physical and spiritual, is it, Sister?"

The beautiful nun simply smiled. The crew brought in large laundry bags.

The first lady came into the room to greet them. "You are early today," she said. "Where is Father Francisco?"

---

[21]   Divine grace

Sister Patricia repeated the story about Francisco's trip to the Vatican and explained their presence as substitutes once more. The first lady walked over to the nun and put an arm around her shoulder. "Please, Sister," she said, "all I ask of you is what I always ask Father Francisco. Please don't disclose where this gift comes from. No matter how much I try to help people, my political enemies try to distort my intentions and my taste, accusing me of spending too much money on luxuries. The socialists and the extreme left in this country don't allow anyone to enjoy the fruits of their work in peace. It's funny and hypocritical, because whenever *they* take it from other people, it's perfectly all right."

The nun replied, "We will not publicize the good actions or this beautiful gesture of your donation. Those lovely dresses will probably be sold and the money used to feed the poor. We know how your enemies work, so that is why we maintain secrecy in everything."

Father Alberto asked Margarita, "I'm sorry to interrupt you, but may I use your restroom?"

Margarita raised her hand, "Sure, sure." She beckoned to another serving woman. "Sylvia, please show Father Alberto to the bathroom."

Sylvia pointed it out to the priest, who bowed and thanked her. He picked up some laundry bags, some partially filled with clothes, some empty, and headed in the direction she had indicated. As he walked to the restroom, he noticed Sylvia disappear behind him.

He carefully slipped a dart gun from his waistband. He entered the restroom and made certain the dart gun was loaded and ready for use. He urinated and flushed the toilet in order to make certain that anyone who might be listening heard the sounds.

Father Alberto was, in reality, one of my most trusted freedom fighters—Elizabeth's brother Hernesto. A thin, wiry man with glasses when not disguised as a balding priest, he had an unassuming air. Yaneba, the beautiful blonde posing as Sister Patricia, was a childhood friend of mine from Cuba. She was the sole survivor of an attack by Castro against her family as they tried to escape when he came into power. Justo was another local freedom fighter I used when I needed someone with intimate regional knowledge to help me in operations there.

Two doors led into the restroom—the one Hernesto had entered from the hallway and the one by which he exited, which led to another hallway. He acted as if he knew exactly where he was going and what he was doing. He walked until he found a door leading into an office. Keeping the dart gun close to his side in concealment, he entered the office. A woman sporting short black hair with a white streak sat behind the desk. She held one hand on a ten-key office calculator as she worked on some accounts.

She looked up in surprise as she saw him. She nervously asked, "Can I help you?"

She reacted quickly as Hernesto brought his hand up. She could tell something was not right—the dart gun didn't have the profile of a gun, precisely, but it certainly didn't look like anything a priest might be expected to carry.

In desperation, she reached under the desk where she kept a concealed revolver attached to the bottom. Before she could get it clear, Hernesto fired two darts. One flew into her face, the needle sticking into her forehead, right between her eyes. The second dart lodged in her cheek bone. The toxin they were tipped with paralyzed her at once, and she fell rigidly back into her chair, her eyes staring vacantly before her and her mouth open as if to speak.

Hernesto quickly concealed the dart gun and unfolded a laundry bag. He managed to get her body inside the bag, and then slid it out into the hallway next to the other bags of clothing. He walked back to the bathroom and went through the opposite door into the living room. Farewells were being said, and Margarita came over to the hallway where the bags of clothing had been deposited and helped load them into the van.

A guard came over and asked, "Do you need any help, Father?"

Hernesto replied, "No, thank you. God bless you, my son."

Hernesto, Yaneba, and Justo got into the van and it pulled slowly away. In the rearview mirror, they could see Margarita waving her arms as she ran up to them. They stopped.

"Father Alberto," she said, "you forgot your rosary in the bathroom and a small bag of clothes!"

Hernesto smiled and said, "Oh, thank you, my daughter." He took the rosary from Margarita, and they loaded the last bag into the van.

They said their farewells, and Hernesto drove towards the gate. After they had cleared the gate, he drove to the end of the block and parked. It was a very wealthy neighborhood, and the spot he had selected was unobtrusive. He removed a manila envelope and removed the photos. He took the image of the short-haired woman and marked an X in red ink over it. "One down," he said. They all checked their watches.

Hernesto drove to a small church nearby and let Justo out. He then drove the van back, parking it outside another manor which held a good view of the mansion they had just left. He pulled a sheet of paper out of his briefcase, consulted it, and checked his watch once more. "We're right on schedule," he said to Yaneba.

They pulled out binoculars to maintain surveillance on the mansion. After they had watched for a little while longer, they saw a man who matched one of the other photos leave the mansion. He carried a suitcase. He walked up to a car and opened a door. He put the suitcase in the passenger's seat and opened it. He pulled out a pistol and checked to make sure it was loaded. He then screwed a silencer on to the muzzle. He closed the suitcase, got into the car, and drove off.

Hernesto casually pulled out of the parking lot and tailed him at a safe distance. The man stopped at the church and walked inside. He dipped his hand in the holy water font and crossed himself before entering the confessional. After a short while, the priest inside said to him, "Go home and pray the Our Father ten times before you sleep tonight. Rest in peace."

There were three muffled shots, and Justo emerged, pulling the body out of the confessional. He motioned to Hernesto, who pulled up by the church. The three of them loaded the body into the van.

A man passing by saw them in the process of loading. He came up and asked, "Is Father José here today?"

"Yes, sit down inside, my son," said Justo. "He should be back in a little while."

Hernesto, Justo, and Yaneba climbed into the van. Yaneba sat in the driver's seat this time as Hernesto pulled out another photo and crossed it out. "So far, so good," he said. "Only one left."

A few hours later, they were in the parking lot of the race track, watching a man in a blue suit with binoculars standing excitedly, cheering on one of the horses. Moments later, he sat down angrily as he ripped up his ticket and threw it on the floor. He stamped away towards the parking lot. He walked up to a black Lincoln Continental and sat down in it. He buckled his seatbelt and was about to start the car when an arm wrapped around his forehead and a muzzle pressed into his neck.

Another muffled shot, and Justo, still wearing his priestly garb, exited the Lincoln. He tucked his pistol away as Yaneba backed the van up to the car and Hernesto hopped out with another bag. Justo and Hernesto stuffed the body into the bag and put it in the back with the others. As they did, Yaneba got out of the driver's seat wearing gloves and holding a towel. She proceeded to thoroughly wipe down the Continental, and she noticed on the floor of the car two unspent rounds of ammunition. They caught her attention because they were long rounds that would fit a rifle, not the kind of pistol this man was carrying.

Yaneba looked at the passenger side front seat and the back seat but saw no rifle. She walked around and opened the trunk. There inside she found the rifle, complete with a telescopic sight, the kind that snipers use. She turned and gestured to Hernesto. "I think we found the guy who killed that poor taxi driver in front of the embassy," she said as he came over. She handed him the rounds. "I'll bet if we do a ballistics check on these and compare with the forensic report, we'll get a match."

Yaneba shut the trunk and went back to her cleaning. When she was finished, she tossed the gloves and towel into the back and got into the driver's seat. As she started the van, Hernesto marked through the final photo. "That's the last one. Let's hope there aren't any others coming behind him." The car phone in the van rang. Hernesto answered it, "Hello, my sister. Everything is fine. Yeah, everything is just dandy and clean as a whistle. You can make your call. The threat no longer exists, and the hunters have been hunted down."

"What time is it?" she asked.

Hernesto checked his watch, and Yaneba cut in, "Tell Elizabeth she owes me a bottle of Dom Pérignon."

Hernesto smiled and rolled his eyes. "Did you hear that, Elizabeth?"

"Yeah, yeah, yeah" Elizabeth replied. "Good work, and congratulations, guys. Ask Yaneba if I get to drink a little of that champagne."

Hernesto replied, "I don't see any problem with that." He looked up at Yaneba. "Is that OK with you if she has a little to drink, since she lost to you?"

Yaneba rolled her eyes and smiled. "Of course. Our friend should be happy and pleased to receive this news. Tell him we will see each other soon. And tell your sister to put that champagne on ice."

Hernesto said goodbye and hung up. It began to rain.

Chapter 10

THE PURSUIT OF OUR TARGETS

Meanwhile, at Robert's house, Zuyen and I were lying in front of the fireplace, celebrating the success of my team with a couple of glasses of champagne. I pulled an envelope out of my coat and handed it to her. "We'll see each other probably in a week in St. Martin's. I have to leave for Los Angeles tonight, but in that envelope you have the instructions for entering the alarm code as well as a key to the house. You should arrive before me, so make yourself comfortable. The tickets for the plane are also in there."

She said, "I'm very excited. I know we'll have a good time there." She filled our glasses once more as the phone rang.

I answered it. "Hi, Elizabeth."

How are you doing?" she asked.

"Unbelievably good," I replied, "like a *como guarapo frio en noche de verano*[22]."

She said, "You are a Cuban for sure!"

"I carry my nationality with pride," I replied, and we both laughed. "You guys did excellent work."

---

[22]   Cold sugar cane juice on a hot summer's night

"Well, I didn't do that much this time," she said, "but I have my grain of sugar in the mix."

"You guys are always efficient and to the point," I told her. "We will have dinner here at eight o'clock tonight before I leave for L.A. Please tell O'Brien to have the tickets ready."

"He probably already has the tickets in his pocket."

"I know," I replied. We said our goodbyes and hung up.

I checked one of my watches and saw it was 6:00 p.m. I looked at Zuyen and ran my fingers through her hair. "Why don't we go to my room? I have a couple of phone calls to make, and then we can get to know each other a little better." That last was almost whispered in her ear, and we both smiled as we walked away with our glasses of champagne in our hands. We exchanged a quick kiss and went upstairs to my room.

Once we were inside, she put the champagne bottle in an ice bucket, and went into the bathroom to change her clothes. When she came out, she was wearing one of my black silk shirts. I had already started to make my phone calls.

She said, "I'm going to take a shower."

I replied, "I will be with you in a minute."

I could see her through the door as she went inside to take a shower. I finished my phone calls and removed my clothes before walking in to join her. As I entered, she was smiling in the shower and beckoned to me seductively. I opened the door to the shower, walked in, and embraced her. We kissed under the water as we began to make love.

A few hours later, O'Brien, Elizabeth, and the rest of my team were with me at the house. The servants, directed by Thomas, were so efficient that our plates and glasses were always filled.

I said to the ambassador, "My friend Robert, did you want to be the first to call the president and tell him that he can brush his teeth in comfort, because everything has been taken care of?"

He looked around at everyone for confirmation, stopping at O'Brien. "Are you guys telling me that there's no longer any danger? Everything is under control?"

O'Brien nodded. "Yes. These guys don't joke around. When you give them the green light for something, it's a green light." I smiled. "Well, the danger is never completely gone, but it's under control."

Elizabeth also smiled. "We should be optimistic. We always have some danger in our lives, but we can say for a while, at least, that the president and his family can sleep in peace."

Robert exclaimed, "Oh, my God! Thank you very much. This man is not just a politician, he's also a decent man, a family man. I only hope that whoever succeeds him in the future has the same values and follows his example."

"Yes, I agree—but don't forget, he is currently the president of this country. Millions of people have entrusted their security to him; that is what we're trying to protect. I want to remind all you guys that someone risked his life in order to bring this information to us in time. Mention that to the president, as well. Keep it in mind. Those people don't get to celebrate with champagne like we're doing now, and they're the most important keys to the success of our work."

Hernesto said, "We should raise our glasses to those people."

"I agree," I said. "You beat me—I was just about to propose that."

O'Brien said, "We should raise our glasses to the people who are trying to stop terrorist acts all over the world, at the gravest risk to their own security as well as that of their families."

We all raised our glasses in toast and saluted these silent warriors. The ambassador smiled and said, "With all my respect to those people and all the credit they deserve, I want to raise a glass to you guys. If I have any problems, I want to have you guys by my side."

We all smiled, and I said, "Well, we'll always be there for you, Robert. All you have to do is ask."

Robert stood up and walked around the table, shaking everyone's hand in turn. O'Brien said, "Don't forget, Mr. Ambassador, that the president of this country owes you a big one. This isn't part of your job—you've gone way above and beyond the call of duty. The people in your profession don't ordinarily get dirt under their nails or their noses too dusty, and yet this is what you've done in these past several hours."

Elizabeth said, "I propose our next toast should be to the ambassador."

Robert said, "Oh, no—please. I didn't do anything. All I did was use the facilities of the United States of America."

Yaneba replied, "Mr. Ambassador, let's hope that the next presidents we have do the same and let us use their facilities."

Robert nodded. "Yeah, you're right." He signaled to Thomas, who brought a portable telephone to him. As he dialed, he said, "Excuse me." He pressed a button on the unit to activate the speakerphone.

A lady on the other end said, "*Hola.*"

"Yes," Robert said. "May I speak with the president, please?"

"Who is this, please?"

"The ambassador of the United States, Robert Budrous."

The lady replied, "Yes, Mr. Ambassador, one moment, please."

A short time later, the president said, "Hello, my friend Robert. How are you doing?"

"Fine, Mr. President. I'm here at my house with my daughter, Dr. Valentine, and a few of his friends, having dinner."

"Oh, that's very nice. Please say hello to everyone for me."

Robert said joyfully, "I have great news for you, Mr. President. Dr. Valentine has given me the honor to be the first to tell you that you do not have to rinse your toothbrush to brush your teeth tonight."

He exclaimed in a surprised voice, "My God! It's already done?"

Robert replied, "Yes, my friends just informed me that the tropical storm that was supposed to come from Cuba over the Gulf of Mexico has changed course and the skies are now clear. It should be a great, sunny day with clear skies tomorrow morning."

The president replied, "You are absolutely sure that no other extreme weather is in the forecast?"

Robert said, "Yes, absolutely sure. If you want, you can speak with Dr. Valentine. He can give you a better reading of the whole picture."

"Yes, I would like to thank him personally, please. Do you mind?"

"Oh, no! Of course," Robert said. "He is here, and he can hear you, sir. We're on the speaker."

"Yes, Mr. President," I said. "How are you doing this evening?"

"Much better after this great news," he replied. "I have to thank you again two times now."

"You don't," I said. "Everything has been taken care of, and it's the pleasure of my friends as well as myself to be at your service."

There was emotion in his voice when he spoke. "Of course I have to thank you and your friends, for your efficiency and quick response to the situation, but also on behalf of my family. I have good news for you as well. I think we have the reason you asked for in our meeting. The project is already in place and will be completed very soon. You'll read about it in the papers once it happens."

I said, "This is wonderful, Mr. President. That means you can send your message loud and clear to your 'Cuban friends.'"

"Yes, and thank you again, Dr. Valentine. Please, the next time you come to Mexico, call me directly. I want you to have dinner with my family and me."

"It will be an honor to me," I replied.

"Good luck, and God bless you and all your friends," the president said.

"The same to you, Mr. President. I'm giving you back to the ambassador. You have a good night."

"And you guys have a good dinner," he answered.

The president and Robert said goodbye to each other, and he hung up. Robert said to me, "Dr. Valentine, if you ever decide to change careers, for whatever reason, I always can use an intelligence adviser. You know where you can find me, since I hope to keep you close to me and my family."

I smiled. "Thank you for your offer. I'll keep it in mind."

We all exchanged smiles and finished our dinner. A cordial course was served, and afterwards we said good night to the ambassador. Zuyen kissed her father and said, "I'll be back in a while. I'm going to take them to the airport."

Elisabeth offered to drive. "You guys sit down in the back, and have a little romantic corner back there."

O'Brien sat in the passenger's seat, and we said goodbye to Hernesto and Yaneba. Zuyen and I settled in the back, and Elizabeth drove the Navigator to the airport. It began to rain hard as we drove through the streets of the city. I stared out the window as the raindrops started to hit, looked at Zuyen's face, and then looked forward.

By the time we reached the airport, Zuyen had nestled herself so that she was virtually lying in my lap. I looked at her lovingly and stroked my fingers through her beautiful hair. She looked through the window at the rain drops and raised her hand to slide it through my beard, and then smiled. I glided my finger along her lovely lips and then onto her chin. We looked at each other and smiled warmly. She leaned up to give me a passionate kiss on the lips.

O'Brien turned a little towards the back, saw this, and smiled. "I think our friend is lucky he found for the second time a great love in his life."

Elizabeth looked through the rearview mirror, smiled, and nodded. Zuyen and I ignored them completely. For the moment, the rest of the world ceased to exist.

Once we hit the parking lot, though, O'Brien called us back to Earth by clearing his throat. "We're here at the airport. Sorry to interrupt your romantic time."

We grinned sheepishly, and Elizabeth smiled at us in good humor. I asked O'Brien, "Do you have the tickets? You're not going to tell me you forgot the tickets, are you?"

"Oops!" he said as he patted his pockets in mock alarm. Then he reached into his coat. "No, here they are."

I took the tickets from him and patted him on the shoulder. "You're a very efficient man."

"OK, I agree with you," he said.

"Don't mention it," I joked back. I turned to Zuyen. "I'll see you next week in St. Martin's."

"OK," she said. "Take care of yourself for me, all right?"

"I will," I promised. "You do the same for me."

O'Brien gave Zuyen a strong hug and said, "Thanks for everything. It's a great pleasure to have met you. You and your father are a very rare species, very unique."

Elizabeth also hugged Zuyen. She whispered in her ear, "Don't worry—I'll take care of him. Even better now, because I know you're a good person, and I can see that you love him."

"Thank you," Zuyen said. "God bless you all."

She got into the driver's seat and rolled down the window. I gave her a small kiss through it and stepped back, releasing her hand. She drove slowly off.

"OK, lover," O'Brien said, "we've got to go and get on the plane."

I waved as she left, and she blew a kiss to me. I soon lost her in the airport traffic.

A Special Moment

The most beautiful times of my life have been those when I was in real love, when I have lived in freedom, and when my soul has been completely bonded to God. Those moments, the most special and happy in my life, ironically have come to be the only times my soul, my body, and my mind have been absolutely terrified of dying. Death could come at any moment of the day, and then it takes that beautiful happiness away. But then I realize that true happiness is being only in the hands of God.

Dr. Julio Antonio del Mármol

Chapter 11

MY SMALL SLICE OF PARADISE

St. Martin's Island

View from Safe House in St. Martin's

One week after the meeting with the president of Mexico, I flew to meet Zuyen at my house in the mountains of St. Martin's. It was a large house with a spacious patio surrounded by many fruit trees and flowering trees of different varieties, including my favorite, jasmine. At that altitude, there was a breathtaking view of the ocean that gave you chills as you looked out on its infinite expanse. There were several hammocks on the patio and a beautiful gazebo built of white painted wood with a palm frond roof.

I lay in the double-sized hammock, sipping a glass of mimosa with Zuyen. It was sunny, but there were occasional sprinkles, the raindrops creating rainbows in the bright sunlight. My chimpanzee named Rocco, my beautiful female Akita named Arena, and my old *guacamaya*[23] Lucky Angel surrounded us to devour the pieces of cheese and pretzels that I dropped for them.

Zuyen handed a Mexican newspaper to me. She said, "My father sent me this for you. He said it will be a delight to the pupils of your eyes."

The headline read, "Cubans Arrested in Guadalajara on Charges of Drug Trafficking and Involvement in Assassination Conspiracies. Mexican Relations with Cuba Start to Deteriorate." *La Voz de la Frontera* was the name of the newspaper. I had a bright smile as I looked at it. Our friend had finally found a strong decoy to send a message to the Castro brothers.

Zuyen grinned broadly. "My father was right—it did put a big smile on your face." She reached up and touched my cheek. "You must be very proud."

"A little," I said. My smile faded, and I grew a bit melancholy. "At the same time, I have a lot of frustrations. Everyone in the intelligence community keeps telling me that Castro will be very difficult to take down. He's sitting on a very delicate nuclear arsenal, and no one wants to take the chance of his firing off an intercontinental missile. So, and pardon my French, all we do is little shit. Unless we take him, his brother, and his entire entourage down, we will never end all this terrorism and craziness around

---

[23] macaw

the world. We need to create something big as proof to everyone in the world, so that we can get rid of these people once and for all. I have to go back to Cuba. If I can get my hands on enough evidence, maybe we can create the commotion I'm looking for."

Zuyen looked at me over the rims of her sunglasses. "I'm going to tell you something. I don't think you'll listen, but I'm going to tell you any way. After what happened in the Mexico City Airport, I don't think you should go back to that island. They will be waiting for you everywhere over there. If they've figured out by now that you were the one who frustrated their plans in Mexico, it will be even worse. I think you should send someone else, and they would probably accomplish the same. Why does it have to be you?"

I smiled at her and looked over the rim of my sunglasses. "Honey, I'm the one who has to go because my people in Cuba won't trust anyone coming from here. The relationship I have with them goes back many years. Besides, the person going over there won't be the person you see before you now. When I go in, I'll have a different face, name, and M.O. This time, I won't go through the front door; I'm going to go in through a window. I assure you I'll return with a smile on my face. I've been doing this now almost half of my life. Some people consider me kind of an expert in what I'm doing. Plus, I now have you to come back to."

She smiled and kissed my cheek. "You promise me you'll return safe?"

"I promise, my love."

She tugged at my beard a little. "You'd better." She released my beard, and we kissed as we rolled in the hammock. We made love surrounded by that beautiful scenery.

The next morning, Zuyen was in the kitchen making a salad. I was in the gazebo with the dog and monkey, roasting a suckling pig on the barbeque as I chopped vegetables. Zuyen came back with drinks. I took one and sipped, and nodded in approval. "What is this?" I asked. "This is delicious."

Rocco jumped around as if he wanted some. Zuyen said, "Hey, don't drink it all! Leave me some."

"Oh, I'm sorry, I thought it was all for me." I handed her the half empty glass.

"I'm just kidding. I have a whole pitcher in the kitchen."

"Oh, you got me," I said, and we both laughed.

She said, "I call this drink St. Martin's because I took all the fruit on the patio: mangoes, papaya, bananas, everything around here, blended them, and added some rum to it."

"Oh," I teased, "you've already converted yourself into a Caribbean lady."

I finished my drink and she said, "You want more?"

Lucky Angel interrupted with a squawk. "Oh," I said, "you want juice?" I held my glass before the bird, and it started to drink. I smiled. "She's going to have a very good nap today."

"Good, *awk*! Good," Lucky squawked.

"Yes, you're going to nap very well today," I said. "Bird, you think the juice is a little tart?"

Zuyen pulled a long face. "Oh, you told me a few minutes ago that it was great!"

"I'm just joking with you," I said. "See? I got you, now!" I pulled off a piece of pork and gave it to her. "How do you like this?"

She nibbled at it and her eyes widened. "It's delicious!" she exclaimed.

I cut off a larger piece and put some steamed vegetables around it. We sat down at the table with the bowl of salad she had made. Arena sat by me, waiting for the bones from the pork, which I dropped into a bowl I had set out for that purpose.

Zuyen went inside the house and brought out a couple of coolers. She began to pack up the food and load up the Range Rover. She had Lucky on her shoulder and took Rocco by the hand, while Arena followed at her heels. We drove down to the beach. Once down there, we unloaded the scuba equipment. Rocco followed Zuyen, while Arena followed me. We opened the umbrella and set everything out beneath it. We put on our masks and fins, and then assisted each other with our tanks. We swam out into the crystal clear waters, small schools of fish swimming around me. I opened up a shellfish with my knife, and the small fish darted in to eat. Zuyen smiled, and I handed a mussel to her so that she could feed fish.

We looked down and saw some lobster crawling around on the ocean floor. We decided to leave them alone. I shot a few fish with my spear gun, and a while later we left the water with a small netted sack filled with fish. I said to her, "Go ahead. I have to clean the fish."

While I started to open up a small portable table to clean my catch, she went under the umbrella. She took a banana from the cooler broke it in two, giving one half to Rocco. She called out, "I'm waiting for you to open the wine!"

"Ok," I replied. "I'll be there in a minute."

We spent nearly the entire day on the beach. As dark started to fall, we headed back to the house. Around 9:00 p.m., after we had showered and cleaned up from our outing, I put on a wig and shaved off my beard, leaving only my mustache. I put on my special rearview glasses. Zuyen snuck into the bathroom to see what I was doing. I turned around suddenly.

"Oh, my God!" she exclaimed. "I thought I was sneaking up on you. How did you hear me?"

"I didn't hear you," I explained, "I saw you. Here." I took off my sunglasses and handed them to her to try on.

"Oh, another one of your toys?" she asked as she turned around, keeping her long hair out of the way.

"You can call them toys," I said. "To me, they're survival tools. They've saved my life many times."

Her expression turned to one of worried concern. I was finished putting on my disguise and asked, "If you saw me in the street, would you recognize me?"

She stepped back and looked at me from different angles. "I don't think your own mother would recognize you."

I smiled in satisfaction. "I won't be longer than eight days. I'll see you in Newport Beach." I handed her a manila envelope. "Inside here are the keys to the house. After I come back, I'm going to spend some time with you in Baja California in Mexico. I have a house there and we'll have a good time."

She put her hands on my face. "We don't have to go anywhere. I will be just as happy if we don't go anywhere so long as you come back alive."

"Don't worry, honey," I assured her. "I'll come back in one piece." I waved my hand over my face and body. "I don't want to come back in several pieces that you'll have to put together with crazy glue. Please, stay here for a few more days, enjoy, and then go to the States. You have the whole itinerary in that envelope."

We got into the Range Rover, and she drove me to the coast. A fishing boat was waiting for me off shore—a small dinghy tied to the pier. A smiling black man, my old friend Chopin, greeted me while Zuyen stood, looking a bit sad. I made a little flourish like a magician and handed her a jasmine. "Where did you get that?" she asked with a big smile of surprise.

"I had it hidden up my sleeve all this time." We kissed, and I walked down the pier. Chopin helped me stow my gear aboard the dinghy. I waved goodbye to Zuyen, who waved back as she watched me leave from the shore, and we made our way towards the boat. She looked like she was about to cry.

Havana, Cuba
2:00 a.m.
Havana Riviera Hotel

I had spent two weeks gathering data on the secret plans the terrorists were constructing in Havana with the aid of my uncle, Yein, and the other freedom fighters. We had obtained about 95% of the information we had been seeking. These people were fanatics, and it difficult to bribe them or penetrate their circles; however, we managed to get to one of them. At this point we just needed the how and where behind the multiple attacks they were planning. We were nearing the end of our investigation, and we were interviewing that subject this night.

I was supposed to join Yein at the Coppelia Ice Cream Parlor. Since it was so early in the morning, I decided to walk to our meeting from where I was staying at the Riviera and so avoid taking a taxi. Many taxi drivers worked with the G-2, and so it was highly desirable to keep contact with these individuals to a minimum. I also felt the need for some exercise. I had enjoyed too many excellent meals lately and thought my belly was growing a little round.

As I walked along the Malecón towards 23rd Street where the parlor was located, a police patrol car pulled up and stopped behind me. Even though I was dressed like a tourist, I must have looked suspicious because few people were walking the streets that night.

Unfortunately, I had forgotten my papers back in my suite.

A police officer and his sergeant got out. They weren't particularly friendly, and it was clear they were going to follow the rules exactly by the book. They did not care for the excuse I had offered regarding my documents. I suggested they come back to the hotel so that I could show them my proof.

The sergeant smirked arrogantly and said, "OK, get in the patrol car, and we'll drive you back to the hotel."

I hesitantly got into the car. As they pulled away, I saw that they weren't turning to head towards the hotel. They drove instead towards Vedado.

"Why aren't you taking me to the hotel like you said?" I demanded. "Where are you taking me now?"

He said very nonchalantly, "Don't worry about it. This is a new regulation from the Ministry of the Interior. We have to bring tourists without identification to the police station to fill out some short forms of identification. It won't take more than ten minutes, and we could lose our jobs if we don't. You just have to fill out your name, country of origin, age, et cetera, and we'll make a copy at the station to show we've done our job. Then we'll take you back to the hotel and compare that form with your documents. If both check out, then you will be released with no problems."

"Oh!" I exclaimed. "I'm under arrest?"

"No," he replied, "just routine procedure."

The only reason I had gotten into that car voluntarily was because of the assurance we would go to the hotel. Now I felt I had been trapped, but I had no other choice at this point. We were by now in the police station parking lot with too many witnesses. I had to proceed with them and see what would happen next.

They brought me into the station. The officer asked, "Sergeant, I haven't eaten all day. Do you mind if I go get something?"

"Go ahead," the sergeant said. The policeman left, leaving me alone with his partner in the small room. He put the form in front of me and then left me in the room to work on it.

As I filled out the form, I dwelt on the great mistakes I had made. First, I had left my documents behind. Second, I shouldn't have gotten into the police car, not when I could have put both of them down and then disappeared into the darkness. However, I'd still had some faith in humanity and had thought that they would keep their word. I looked up through the window and saw the sergeant approaching. He had a folder with some papers in one hand and a fingerprinting kit in a large aluminum case in his other. That was not going to be good for me. The hairs on my neck raised.

I went into full alert. The last thing I could allow him to do was to fingerprint me. I rapidly shot out of my chair to hide behind the door jamb. I put my back against the wall and rapidly pulled one of my handkerchiefs out of my pocket, along with a small travel bottle of Grand Marnier. I carefully avoided the fumes of ether that wafted from the bottle as I opened it. I emptied half the contents of the bottle into my handkerchief.

A few seconds passed, and my heart started to pound so loudly that I thought the sergeant would hear me. He reached the door, and I watched the doorknob wiggle as he struggled to open it with both hands full. Finally, the door started to slowly open. I saw one of his legs as he entered the room.

Without hesitating for a second, I jumped behind him, grabbing his neck with my left arm. My right hand clamped the handkerchief against his nose and mouth to force him to inhale the anesthetic. As I did so, I nudged the door shut with one of my feet. The aluminum case of the fingerprinting kit dropped as he struggled to defend himself, so I quickly readjusted my balance to kick my right foot out to intercept the kit before it hit the floor. I winced slightly as the large case hit the bridge of my foot. However, instead of a loud clatter, it slid virtually noiselessly onto the floor.

After a few moments, he was unconscious. It took a few minutes of work to switch our clothing. I put him in my chair, and let his head rest on his arms on the desk, as if he had fallen asleep sitting there. I took the fingerprinting kit and rapidly stuffed the papers scattered on the floor back into the folder, put his hat on my head, and made sure everything was in order. I left the small room, closing the door behind me.

I walked past other policemen bringing in other people. I kept my head down to hide my face. I walked up to an empty desk and put the folder and kit down on it.

A *jineteras*[24] was creating a huge commotion as she was being processed. Several officers tried to get statements from the arresting officers as well as the people they were attempting to book, making the station seem more crowded.

As I passed the desk, one of the officers said, "You have a good night, Sergeant Manrique. You're a lucky man to be going home now."

Without raising my head, I held up my hand to acknowledge him and nodded my head. I continued on my way out the back door. As I left the building, the other policeman came out the door. He was silhouetted by the dim light of lamp over the door. He called after me, "Sergeant! Where did you leave the tourist? I'm going to process him now that I've finished my lunch."

I was completely shrouded by the darkness in the parking lot. I raised my hand in irritation, and I pointed abruptly towards the building as I shook my head angrily. I wanted to convey the impression of a man eager to get off work and go home.

---

[24] prostitute

He hastily nodded his head obediently and said, "*Buenas noches,* Sergeant." He retreated back inside the building.

As soon as I saw he had gone, I walked over to the patrol car in which they had brought me. I checked the uniform belt and found a set of keys there. I looked through them and found one which was inscribed in Cyrillic letters. It could only have been the key for the Russian-made patrol car. I got in, started the engine, and slowly drove out. A couple of patrol cars entered the station, and the officers saluted me as I left and drove onto the avenue.

I went straight to the ice cream parlor and tried to locate Yein's car. I saw her backing out of the parking lot. Perhaps she thought something had happened to me and was going to search for me. I smiled, now more relaxed, and put the roof lights on as I pulled in behind her. She pulled over at once. I got out and walked over to her window.

As soon as she saw me, she breathed an exasperated sigh of relief. "Where have you been, and where did you steal that police car and uniform?"

She smiled as soon as she had vented. "I'm sorry. I couldn't hold him any longer. He took off, assuming the worst."

"When I tell you what just happened, you won't believe it. However, God was with me, and I don't think we'll have any problems for the moment. It won't last, though. We'll have to rush my exit out of Cuba, and you guys can proceed here with our new contact and see what you can get out of him."

"What do you need?"

"Let me park this police car somewhere here. I'll give you the details then of what just happened and what we should do immediately."

I parked the car someplace unobtrusive and got into the passenger seat of her car. She drove towards the Riviera Hotel. She went inside to retrieve my things in case someone was watching for me. She brought them back to the car, and then drove me to her house. On the way, I related my most recent adventure.

"My biggest worry right now," I concluded, "is that I will be identified as soon as they examine the security tapes from the police station cameras."

We arrived at her house, and I took a long shower and changed into the disguise of a very old, overweight man. I looked pretty nasty, but the idea here was to completely throw off anyone who might now be actively searching for me. We ate some fruit and drank the shakes Yein had made, and then she turned on the TV. They already had the face of my old disguise on the news. They stated that I had killed the police sergeant, and that I was wanted dead or alive as a terrorist and the number one enemy of the Revolution. We both shook our heads.

Yein said, "These people don't waste any time to lie and discredit their enemies."

She handed me a DVD case for the movie *Inspector Gadget*. "And so neither can we. I burned all of the data onto two disks while you showered and changed, and I put them in here."

I took the case and nodded. I gestured towards the TV. "I didn't kill him. I left him unconscious. Lies are all we can expect from them."

We left her house and headed towards the Havana harbor. Yein stopped by a newsstand and picked up a copy of *Granma*, the only newspaper published in Cuba. My story was already the front page headline.

She continued into the harbor and parked the car along one of the piers. She introduced me to a man who had been working with them, the captain of a Spanish merchant ship. She hugged me and we kissed each other on the cheek.

"They will drop you at the Cayman Islands as they cruise by them," she told me.

Several hours later, I had changed my disguise once again, and the ship arrived at my drop point off the Caymans. I took a private plane I had pre-arranged, flown by a pilot I had frequently used before, to Baja California in Mexico.

Once at my house in Baja, I had a long, hot bath and a light meal.

Afterwards, I got out my Land Rover jeep and drove towards the Tijuana/San Isidro border crossing and my final destination of Corona del Mar. Six hours later, I took the Jamboree Road exit off of I-405 towards my house in California. All the information I had retrieved in Cuba was perfectly protected and hidden inside my vehicle. I smiled in satisfaction.

I discovered much later that Robert Budrous' most trusted advisor, Damian, had sold his soul to the devil, our enemies. He had intercepted one of the letters Zuyen had sent her father with the address of one of my safe houses.

After I crossed the border from Mexico into the United States, I drove straight to my house in Corona del Mar. Although I had told her I would return in eight days, it had taken me a full two weeks.

Zuyen was thrilled and surprised to see me, as I had not sent word ahead that I was coming. After we spent a few hours catching up and making beautiful love after our long separation, I took a shower. We sat down in the living room afterwards, and I took the DVDs out of my bag. I told her about the DVDs and their importance.

"If anything happens to me," I told her gravely, "get this into O'Brien's hands, and no one else's. The contents are only for his eyes, those of his superior, Addison, and the President of the United States."

Since we had left behind a few dead bodies among our enemies in Cuban intelligence, we in no way wanted to jeopardize the safety of the people who had gotten us access to that conference. I put both disks in the library. I let Zuyen know I was going to run some errands and would return shortly.

Zuyen said, "OK, honey. I'm going to take a shower. I'll be done by the time you get back."

I got out to the Land Rover, but I stopped for a moment. The worst case scenario would be that our enemies would retrieve all of the information I had obtained. It would be more prudent to hide the two disks in separate locations. I turned off the engine and walked back up the driveway.

I went into the atrium and pulled out the *Inspector Gadget* case. I took out one of the disks and walked to the master bathroom to let Zuyen know. However, she was singing happily in the shower, and I decided it could wait. I smiled, turned, and left to run to the bank and a few other errands.

I left the house and thought for a moment where I could stow the disk safely. I already had a decoy planted in the jeep. I smiled and walked back to the license plate.

It was of a design seldom seen in the United States any more, in which the license plate hinged on a spring to provide access to the gas cap in the rear of the vehicle. I pulled the license plate down, revealing the small compartment. I slid the plastic jacket containing the disk inside. I moved the license plate up and down; it was a perfect fit. Even if someone looked for it, no one was going to see what was concealed there.

I drove off towards the bank, and after completing my errands about an hour later, I decided I should bring O'Brien and Elizabeth directly to my house so that I could deliver all of my information into O'Brien's hands in the comfort and security of my home.

Chapter 12

DESPERATE TO SILENCE ME

Gelson's Market, Newport Beach
April 15, 2001
5:30 p.m.

Parking lot where attack took place

I was driving from my house in Corona del Mar in my yellow Defender Land Rover while speaking to Zuyen on the phone. "I'm going bring some lobsters to make a thermidor," I said. "And set out some more plates. I'm bringing our friends O'Brien and Elizabeth over for dinner."

Zuyen said, "OK, I'll make a beautiful seafood salad and a bouillabaisse."

"Great! I'll be home no later than half an hour." I hung up.

As I drove into the parking lot, I noticed two sedans, one olive green and one black, each with a man sitting inside. I locked eyes with the men in each car, and they quickly glanced down as I did so. It gave me a strange feeling, but I didn't let myself get overly concerned. I assumed they were sitting there making cell phone calls.

I saw one man get out of his car as if looking to see where I was going to park. I made it a point to always keep myself aware of my surroundings. Though I was concerned, I walked into the supermarket, making sure to memorize the men's features. I hoped I wouldn't see them again, but it was better to be safe than sorry.

What I did not realize until later was that there were two men in each of those cars, and they later parked on opposite sides of my Land Rover in order to keep it under surveillance from all angles.

The sun was setting over the ocean—a spectacular view from the hillside where the market is situated. Since it was getting a little darker, I took my sunglasses off and put them in my pocket as I walked inside the market. I took a shopping cart and began to load it with various vegetables from the produce aisle. I picked up some tomato sauce and headed to the seafood aisle for caviar and lobster.

As I looked through the seafood, my cell phone rang. "Hello?" I answered.

O'Brien said, "Hello, how are you doing? Is everything OK?"

"Yes, I just arrived. I have the proof with me. We'll meet at my place at eight o'clock."

"Eight o'clock?"

"Yes. We'll have some dinner, and we can talk about the details over that."

"Be careful. What you're bringing us is too valuable, and we cannot afford to lose either you or that information."

"I know. Don't worry about it," I reassured him. "Nobody knows that I'm even here in the country. As always, I came in through Mexico."

"OK. I trust your judgment, but be extremely careful, OK?"

I smiled. "OK, Papa. We'll see each other later. Let's cut this chat short so I can see to it you have good food on the table tonight."

I hung up, and noticed the two men coming towards me. They were dressed in black, wearing dark glasses. It was all too strange. Both of them had empty grocery carts. As soon as they saw me looking at them, they split up and went away in different directions.

I took my time to look through the packages on the seafood display. I put on my special sunglasses and watched them in the special rear vision crystals. I was able to keep them under watch on both sides. I went up to the seafood counter, where John, a gray-haired clerk, greeted me cordially.

"How are you doing, Dr. Mármol? It's been a long time since we've seen each other. Have you been out of town? Taking a long vacation?"

"You're right on both counts, John," I said. "I've been taking a long vacation out of town. It's nice to see you again. You look good—how's your family?"

"We're all well, thanks. My little girl, Jenny, is going to be a sweet sixteen shortly."

"My God! Little Jenny at sixteen—where does the time go, John?"

"Yes," John answered, "don't mention it. As time passes, I get more gray hair and my belly gets bigger. Nothing I can do about it."

"Yes, John," I teased him, "there's something you can do—stop eating!"

He grabbed his belly with both hands. "Do you know how much this cost, and what a big investment I have in this?"

While we spoke so jocularly, John started to scoop up some shrimp. He knew my usual order quite well and started to fill it without asking. "Two pounds?"

"A little more," I said. "We're having guests over, so I don't want to run out."

"How many lobsters?"

"Make it five, please."

John walked over to the live lobster tank, and pulled out some beautiful lobsters to show me. Upon my approval, he began to wrap them up. As he did so, he asked, "When are you going to invite me on one of your great scuba-diving fishing trips? Especially with the great meals you have on your yacht—you still have it?"

"Yes. Possibly next month, since it's my birthday."

He smiled and winked at me as he held up his hand in an "OK" gesture. "Don't forget me, all right? When you invite me, we always have a lot of fun, and whenever you bring me aboard, I bring you luck. We always catch a lot of seafood!"

I smiled. "Yeah, you're right, John, one hundred percent. Whenever you don't come with us, we come back empty and half-drunk."

"You see? You see? I'm telling you!" he exclaimed with a satisfied smile.

He gave me the seafood and I put it in my cart. I made my way towards the cashier. Every register had long lines. One of the men I had seen earlier was in a line near me. A third man, dressed similarly to the other two but with a baseball cap, rammed his cart into the man in line.

That man turned on him violently. "Are you blind or mad? Are you an imbecile? Look at what you did to my shoe!"

This exchange took me by surprise. It was a little over the top, but still pretty natural. It certainly attracted my attention. The man, in the meantime, licked his finger and began to work on the scratch on his shoe to repair the damage done by the shopping cart.

The other man said, "I'm sorry—I wasn't paying any attention at all. I don't even know what I was doing. I'm sorry."

The man looked up from wiping his shoe with a look that could kill, while the other man continued to apologize. They looked at each other as if there was going to be a fight soon. People around them began to get nervous, exchanging worried glances with each other.

I looked at the man with the scratched shoe and shook my head. I moved up to the cashier to pay for my goods. The man with the scratched shoe went up to the next register. He looked at me and asked, "How can anyone be such a moron and so careless?"

I answered, "My friend, it's a small mistake. Just let it go. Down the road, one day, that man will have someone do the same to him, and he will feel the same way you do right now."

The young cashier smiled at me innocently. "Very nicely put, Dr. Mármol," she said. "Forgive and forget."

"Forgive," I said with a smile, "but never forget."

"No?"

"Nope. If you forget, you'll only get hurt again." I picked up my packages and looked at the name tag on her blouse. "Have a good day, Janet. Just remember—forgive, don't forget."

"Thank you, Dr. Mármol," she answered. "Have a good day."

The man with the baseball cap finished at his register at that moment and immediately started to follow me. He walked more quickly than one normally would with a shopping cart, as if he were trying to catch up with me. As he got close to me, I began to get uncomfortable.

"Can you believe that guy?" he asked me. "I didn't do anything to his shoe. You couldn't see anything. Did you see how he behaved? Some people don't have any class at all. Was he stressed out? I don't know what's wrong with people these days."

I nodded as I continued toward the Land Rover. "Forget about it, for God's sake. Just go home. There's more to worry about in life. These things happen." I was watching behind me and saw the other man coming with only a few things in his cart. The man kept trying to engage me in conversation, but I said, "I'm sorry, my car is right here. Have a good evening."

I turned the cart around, so that I would avoid the man by going around the back of my car. I maneuvered between the car to try and put some distance between us. The man, however, turned down another row, virtually following me. I assumed his car was parked near to mine.

Suddenly and out of nowhere, the man with the scratched shoe blocked me with his cart as he emerged from another row. I was stuck between their two carts. I backed up to let him pass, and went towards the passenger door to unload my groceries.

The man with the shoe yelled at the other, "You idiot! How would you like it if I did the same thing to you and rammed my cart into yours?" He ran his cart with all his strength, but instead of hitting the other man's cart, he rammed my car, scratching the splatter guard with a long gouge.

Angrily, I said, "Hey, my friend, look at what you just did to my car! You're just aggravating the whole thing. For God's sake, just let it go!"

He said, "Oh, I'm sorry—I didn't want to do it to your car, just his cart." He abandoned his cart to approach me.

I stepped back to defend myself, but felt a touch on my right shoulder. I started to turn, but was punched very solidly in my forehead by a hand wearing brass knuckles. I dropped to the ground in a semi-conscious state, stunned.

Two other men appeared, moving in a rapid, professional manner. They began to strike me with telescoping nightsticks. Meanwhile, the other two began to search the Land Rover. It became apparent that they weren't finding what they were looking for. I saw one man pull out a gun and the unmistakable pipe of a silencer, which he started to screw on to the muzzle.

"I can't find anything in here!" one man yelled.

Another voice said, "It has to be there!"

The same man said, "No, there's nothing here."

One of the men hitting me left to join the search. Everything seemed to move in slow motion for me, due to the beating I was taking. The man with the pistol put the muzzle next to my right ear. He said, "Well, say your last prayer, fucker."

"Wait!" one of the men yelled. "We can't find anything. We might need him. Don't shoot him yet."

The man with the pistol said, "We've already wasted too much time and created too much commotion."

I was tapped with the nightstick, but I didn't move, pretending to be completely unconscious, my eyes slightly open. The tip of the pistol left my head. An elderly couple saw the situation. The woman put her hands to her mouth and yelled, "Oh, my God! What are you doing to that man?"

I opened my eyes fully to see better what was going on, and I saw the man shoot the woman in the head, her lifeless body falling to the ground a few feet from me. The old man tried to hold her as one of the other men went around and shot him in the back of the head.

Quickly, as if they did this every day, the other two came around, picked up the bodies, and put them into the trunk of one of the sedans. Then they returned to their search of the Land Rover. It was all like a drug-induced nightmare for me, as if a large snowball were rolling down a mountainside before my eyes. Except in my mind, the snowball reduced, and as it did so, my vision cleared.

I was still dizzy and tried to rub my eyes. I saw them pulling up the floor mats. No one had bothered to search me, and I felt my 9mm Brazilian Taurus inside my jacket. I still lacked the hand strength to grasp the pistol, so I flexed my hand several times to get some feeling back into it. Finally, I felt enough strength to grab it, and I drew my pistol.

I could feel blood on my face, probably from the beating. I could clearly see one of the men removing the cover from the spare tire of the Land Rover. He found some diskettes and microfilm in a magnetic box affixed to the wheel.

He smiled in satisfaction and raised his voice to the others. Before he finished saying anything, he walked towards me, pistol in hand to finish me off. He put it on my forehead, but with my left hand I pushed his gun away from his body. The shot rang out and hit one of the cars nearby. At the same time, I shot three times into his jaw. Pieces of brain and skull flew through the air. The recoil snapped him away from me. The other men heard the shots and started to run towards me in confusion. The man with the baseball cap ran in front of me to see what had happened, while another of the men saw me through the window as I struggled to my feet. He hastily pulled his gun and fired, but the man with the baseball cap ran in front of him and was hit instead.

I fired four more times. The larger man, who had found my hidden magnetic box, fell to the ground, with two bullet holes in his forehead and two in his chest. The other man dived to the ground to snatch the magnetic box as it skittered underneath my car. I fired twice more, this time missing the man and hitting the tires. He rolled underneath the Land Rover, abandoning his search. He sought escape by ducking underneath another car.

I couldn't get a clear shot, and pain shot through my leg as I tried to stand. Apparently, it had been broken during the beating. I started to drag myself over the greasy pavement towards the Land Rover. I knew I had to get away.

I had lost visual contact with the other two men. I was also aware that my gun only held thirteen bullets, one more than the recommended load. I was down to four rounds, two for each of the men. I continued to crawl and shot twice to distract them.

A crowd had gathered, and people screamed for the police as they scattered. I was bloody and dirty, and still had no idea where the other men were. I no longer cared about hurting them. I needed to get myself to safety. I could hear police and paramedic sirens approaching and knew this wasn't going to be good. I didn't have a license to carry a gun, for one thing.

I crawled over and retrieved the magnetic box. Gun in one hand and the box in the other, I used my elbows to drag myself to the curb marking the border of the lot. I hoped I could at least get a clear view of anyone approaching me and defend myself if need be. The low wall of the building served as protection for my back, and the corner in which I wedged myself was the best defense under the circumstances.

It was apparent that the other two men no longer wished to pursue me, but as I looked up I saw immediately in front of me a pair of black pants and shoes. I tried to train my pistol up to shoot the figure, but my vision was still blurred. A voice stopped me.

"No, Dr. Mármol, it's John. Don't shoot. You're badly hurt."

"John. Help me. Someone attacked me and beat me up." I could barely make out the white apron John wore. I lowered my pistol. "Please, put this pistol away. Don't let anyone know about it or see it, please."

I handed him the magnetic box. "Also, please put this in a secure place."

He took the pistol and the box from my hand. He said, "Don't worry, my friend, no one will see either of these items." I could barely hear what he said as he put both into his pockets.

The paramedics put me on a stretcher, and from that vantage I could see the police questioning everyone in the area. A lieutenant walked up to John and took some notes as he asked questions. Police collected bullet cartridges from the ground—however, there were no dead bodies. Only I was there to be loaded into an ambulance. As they did, I lost consciousness.

Chapter 13

THE TREASON IN OUR RANKS AND MY TEMPORARY WITHDRAWAL

Hoag Hospital

*Z*uyen, Elizabeth, and O'Brien sat in the waiting room at Hoag Hospital. John was also there with his wife. After several hours of surgery, I was moved to the Intensive Care Unit. Two doctors and a nurse walked into the waiting room, and Zuyen and O'Brien stood to speak to him.

"How is he, Doctor?" Zuyen asked.

The doctor replied, "He's stable. I'm the brain surgeon, Dr. Raymond. This is my colleague, Dr. Tosca, an orthopedic surgeon. Dr. Mármol's prognosis is not very good. He's semi-comatose. He has a very severe concussion as well as a brain clot. We've treated the clot. Now let's hope that another doesn't form in the next twenty-four hours."

Zuyen tried to hold back her tears. Elizabeth tried to keep control, but two tears rolled down her cheeks as she shook her head.

"He has four broken ribs and a broken leg with two fractures, one near his ankle and one close to his knee," Dr. Tosca said. "His jaw has been fractured as well. It's not too bad, but it's still a jaw fracture. He also has a fractured ulna in his right arm."

"We also have to hope that he doesn't have a detached retina," continued Dr. Raymond, "or he might go blind in the future."

At this, Zuyen broke down wept openly.

"He should be very happy to be alive," Dr. Raymond finished. "He's a very strong, physical man. Let's wait and hope he can survive these injuries."

He indicated the nurse standing with them. "Cathy will take you to see him. Let me warn you that he's not completely conscious, and we cannot move him. The hematoma doesn't make him look too pretty, but at least he's alive and stable." He put his hand on Zuyen's shoulder. "Let's pray to God for him. That's all we can do now."

The surgeons left the room. Cathy asked Zuyen, "Do you want something to drink, honey? Are you OK?" Zuyen shook her head. "Do either of you want anything?" O'Brien and Elizabeth shook their heads.

"Are you ready to see him?" My friends nodded, and Cathy took them to the room where I lay semi-conscious but unable to speak.

They looked at me. Elizabeth said, "I barely recognize him with all those bandages."

Cathy put a wet towel on my head. Zuyen asked, "May I do that?"

"Sure," Cathy said. "Sometimes patients in this stage can see and hear but they can't communicate."

Zuyen started to wipe my forehead. "Honey, if you can hear me, we're here for you. You'll be OK. You're a very strong man."

A few hours passed. John and his wife said their goodbyes and left.

"We have to have faith," Elizabeth said to Zuyen. "We have to thank God that he's alive. That's the most important thing."

"I know, I know." Zuyen started to cry on Elizabeth's shoulder.

After a while, everyone had calmed down. I saw O'Brien signaling two men at the door, and they walked out. It was apparent that he had organized a guard for me. Zuyen gave O'Brien a kiss on the cheek. "Thank you."

"It's the least I can do for him," O'Brien said, "give him some protection. We have to make sure those people don't come back and finish him."

Zuyen bit her lip as if remembering something. O'Brien, of course, noticed, and said, "What?"

"You said these guys want to finish him? He told me when he got back into the country that if something bad happened to him or if he lost his life, I was to give you a DVD." She put her hand over her mouth as if she were about to cry again.

O'Brien's eyes widened in shock. "When did he tell you that?"

"Oh, my God, this afternoon."

O'Brien held her hand. "Oh, good—thank you. If that is what I think, he knew someone was following him already. I told him to be careful today. You know how he is: he doesn't give things like that any importance."

"Don't be so hard on him. He pretends like that so that you won't worry, but he's already taken his precautions."

O'Brien took a moment to regain his composure. "Where is the DVD?"

"At home."

O'Brien snatched out his cell and made a call, giving my address to the person on the other end of the line. "Please move quickly. They might already be on the way over there." He held Zuyen's shoulder and said to her and Elizabeth, "Let's go to the house immediately."

"Yes, I'll take you there. He warned me that nobody but you should see this DVD."

O'Brien squeezed her hand. "Don't worry, Zuyen. It will be the way he wants it."

Zuyen gave me kiss on the cheek before the three left.

They left the hospital in a black Lincoln Navigator that was waiting for O'Brien. A large man, at least 6'4" with the body of a weightlifter, green eyes, and dark skin opened the back doors for the ladies. He then opened the passenger door for O'Brien with a great deal of respect. After closing the door, he scanned the area for anything suspicious.

He got into the driver's seat and said, "The nurse gave this to me. I believe this is Dr. Mármol's cell phone. She said they found it in the ambulance."

O'Brien pointed to Zuyen. The man handed her the phone, and she said, "Thank you."

The man started the car and they left the hospital followed by another Navigator. Zuyen stared out the window as the rain hit the windshield, mirroring her tears. She put her hand to her mouth as she tried to control her emotions.

The driver repeatedly looked at Zuyen through the rearview mirror. Elizabeth held Zuyen's hand and continuously handed her tissues from a box. Zuyen crossed her legs, exposing her thighs, which was noticed appreciatively by the driver.

A car quickly switched lanes, and the driver had to swerve into another lane to avoid the collision. "Sorry, everybody. Some moron in a Porsche nearly put us in an accident."

Elizabeth tensely replied, "Maybe if you were watching the road instead of the rearview mirror, that wouldn't have happened. Maybe you'll show some respect and we'll get to where we're going in one piece." She reached over to fix Zuyen's dress.

Zuyen quickly rearranged herself, shooting a nasty look at the driver. O'Brien realized what was going on and looked straight ahead in rebuke. The driver, like a kid with his hand caught in the cookie jar, quickly adjusted the mirror.

When they drove up to the house, Zuyen pressed the button to the gate and they entered. They drove up the circular driveway, followed by the other Lincoln. They got out and O'Brien gave the guards from the other car the order to stick around. He spoke into his radio, and additional guards took position.

A beautiful weeping willow stood outside the house, and Roman planters containing palms stood on either side of the door. O'Brien and Elizabeth went inside, and separately swept each side of the house with guns drawn. Once they knew it was clear, they brought Zuyen inside. She walked into the atrium, which was made of black aluminum bars and heavily tinted glass that allowed one to see out but not in. She entered the library, which was filled with DVDs and VHS tapes. Everyone sat down on a large white leather sofa, as Zuyen went through the DVDs to pull out *Inspector Gadget*. She put it in the DVD player, and my face came on the screen, holding up the picture of a terrorist.

"Number one, Ahsan Ahmed. I have irrefutable evidence in my possession that he has been training in Cuba under military experts in high explosives and chemical weapons. They have also been training him in guerrilla warfare. The Cuban government has given him in excess of $175,000 as well as a certain amount of Canadian money—we don't know how much. If you remember, he was supposed to go from Canada to Los Angeles, but we arrested him at the ferry border crossing in New York, diverting his mission, which was to blow up a sizeable portion of the Los

Angeles Airport. If he failed in that, his plan B was the Orange County Airport or plan C at the Ontario Airport. As we all know, he is a high-level operative for al-Qaeda and has very strong ties with Osama bin Laden.

"All of these people come in and out of Cuba like a 24-hour convenience store with a gas station, filling their tanks with money, shelter, and food, taking military classes in terrorist tactics, and receiving instruction in the most sophisticated techniques in manufacturing explosives and how to place them for maximum impact in terms of destruction and loss of life. This has become the new guerrilla warfare, passed along from Ché Guevara's famous booklets, updated for the modern fighter for use in destroying the large democratic metropolises around the world."

I held up another picture. "Meged Moged. This individual is already in the United States. He is the brother of Ahsan Ahmed. This is new information that I will show you. These men have spent at least a year, if not longer, preparing for what they call 'the Great War.' These men have not only been received in glory as heroes in Cuba, but they have also been treated like royalty. At the same time, they have received all the logistical training I mentioned, in addition to training in biological and chemical weapons.

"Then they are sent to the United States to locations like San Diego, Arizona, New Jersey, and Miami and Delray Beach in Florida. Look for the Yanni CDs, *In Celebration of Life* and *Dare to Dream*. In those cases, you will find more detailed descriptions as well as the assumed names they are currently using in the United States, as well as whatever data we have on al-Qaeda. The data will not match because they are using false identities, but you'll still be able to make facial matches based on the information I give to you."

O'Brien looked at the others, and they all exchanged looks of disbelief.

"Saving the best for last," I continued, "there is a very strong possibility of multiple simultaneous attacks at several airports across the United States. That is their ultimate plan. Some of these people are already inside. Others will enter the United States from different points of entry. They will then infiltrate their way into different states.

"You guys should be working in conjunction with the FBI and any other agency you can reach. If possible, get the president's immediate attention to bypass the normal established bureaucracy and their accompanying impediments. Have him arrange indictments on any excuse that can be fabricated just to see if any of them cracks and tells the truth. That is our only hope.

"They call this operation 'the Big One.' We don't know exactly what they have in mind, but whatever it is, it will be huge with repercussions all over the world. They have kept all of this extremely confidential. We have been trying very hard to get close to any one of these people, but so far, there's been a block of iron in our way. All we have gotten from them so far is that they will bring the United States to their knees. Like in a Trojan Horse, they will sneak in and burn to the ground the heart of the U.S.A."

I held up a drawing of a Trojan horse with figures creeping out of it at night. "This is extremely delicate, as some of them are already in place inside the U.S. We don't know why, but they have all been trained inside Cuba to fly airplanes. Let's hope we're not too late. God help us if we are."

The DVD ended and the image went to a color bar with the sine wave tone sounding through the speakers. Zuyen got up and removed the DVD, replaced it in its case, and handed it to O'Brien. She said, "Please, make sure this doesn't fall into the wrong hands. I'm only repeating what he told me to tell you."

She looked through the music collection for the two Yanni disks I had mentioned. "Oh, my God!" Zuyen exclaimed. "They're not here! Maybe he felt something was wrong, and he moved them to a different place."

O'Brien scratched his eyebrows. "I think so, it's possible. It sounds like him. He knows how important this is. Do you have any idea where he might have put them?"

Zuyen shook her head. "I have no idea. All I can suggest is that we search the house."

O'Brien replied, "I don't think he'll just have them lying around the house, but let's take a look."

"Why don't you guys check around the kitchen, and I'll check in the master bedroom?"

The three of them separated and began their search. After Zuyen finished in the master bedroom, she walked into the office. It had a bay window constructed of the same materials as the atrium, and through it she could see that the lights in the driveway were on.

She saw a car with four men blocking the exit to the driveway. They looked like they might be O'Brien's people. She looked down at his bodyguards inside and saw that they were lying in awkward positions against the car. The large one that looked like a bodybuilder was struggling with the men, striving to close the gate as the others pulled the dead bodies inside the cars. One man appeared to be in charge and gestured for others to go around the house.

Elizabeth walked up to Zuyen, who motioned for silence as she emphatically pointed out the window. Elizabeth grimly nodded and pulled her gun out. "Follow me," she said very softly.

The front doorbell rang, and O'Brien walked over towards it. "Who is it?" he asked.

The bodybuilder said, "Addison is here, and he wants to talk to you."

Elizabeth darted up to O'Brien and whispered in his ear. O'Brien nodded. He stepped away from the door. "OK. Let them in, Elizabeth." He pulled his pistol and loaded it.

Elizabeth unlocked the door slowly. She turned the knob to release the catch, and flung it open even as she jumped back. Both Elizabeth and O'Brien opened fire simultaneously, and the two men dropped dead, each shot in the head. To make sure, they both stepped forward and fired aimed shots into their skulls.

The other men in the driveway took cover and opened fire— the silencers on their weapons making a distinctive popping sound with the whine of the bullets the only indication of the real threat. O'Brien was hit in the shoulder and dropped his pistol.

He stumbled back to give Elizabeth a clear shot. She fired twice, hitting the gunman in the throat and head. The men in the back of the house started to shoot through the sliding glass door. The glass on the door shattered. The wildly aimed shots ripped through and broke several wine glasses that hung over the bar in the living room.

Zuyen quickly shut and locked the front door, even as Elizabeth whirled to shoot back at the men in the rear. She slid on her belly across the piano and dove onto the marble floor. She rolled up and shot one of the men down. She said to Zuyen, "Get O'Brien into the Navigator!"

Zuyen went through the bodybuilder's pockets and retrieved the keys. She activated the remote on the gate, but nothing happened. The bullets from the rear of the house continued their assault. Zuyen struggled to get O'Brien into the Navigator.

Still shooting as she ran, Elizabeth sprinted and jumped into the Navigator. Seeing the gate wasn't opening, she stomped down on the accelerator and rammed through both the gate and the car blocking it. They could no longer hear the pop of the silenced weapons, but the sound of bullets ricocheting around them alerted them that they were still under fire.

The tires squealed as the Navigator's wheels spun, and the smell of burning rubber assailed their noses. Two men emerged from either side of the house. One of them took careful aim at Elizabeth as she backed up to make another ramming attempt. She saw him and swerved wildly towards him. To avoid being hit, he jumped out of the way, diving into the bougainvillea in the planter beside the pavement. She rammed once more, this time clearing a slight passage, and she was able to swerve to the left and out onto the street.

"Elizabeth, he's bleeding a lot," Zuyen said. She removed O'Brien's shirt in order to apply a makeshift pressure bandage on his wound.

Elizabeth floored it and drove rapidly through the streets.

"Slow down, Elizabeth," O'Brien said. "I don't think they're going to take this into the streets. The last thing we need is to be stopped by a patrol car and have to explain all of this."

Zuyen said, "I don't think they hit any major blood vessels or organs. It looks like they got the top of your shoulder." She folded his shirt several times and applied pressure. She pulled a couple of scrunchies from her hair and wrapped them around the bandage. "The most important thing here is to stop the bleeding."

She helped him sit up in his seat and held his good hand over his injury. "Put pressure there as best you can."

O'Brien's phone rang. Instinctively, he reached for it, but grimaced in pain. Zuyen picked it up and held it to his ear. She could hear a man's voice say, "O'Brien, our man is up. The doctors just informed us he just regained consciousness. They can't believe it. They said that if this happened, you had instructed them to inform you immediately. He's asking for Zuyen and you."

O'Brien replied, "Yes, thank God. Make sure *nobody* gets in that room, even if you have to barricade yourself in there. Tell him to hang in there. We're on our way." He looked at Zuyen. "Good news. Julio Antonio has awakened from his semi-comatose state."

Zuyen started to cry in relief and crossed herself. O'Brien shook his head. "I have to tell you, there's no doubt in my mind that this man is one of the Chosen Ones. Following God's command to help those who help themselves, we have to get him out of the hospital, no matter what the doctors say. We have *got* to get him to a safe location. This is too big, and these people won't stop until they finish him off."

"Yes," Zuyen said, "after what just happened at the house, I don't think anyone is safe in any of our usual locations."

Elizabeth said, "We have to move him out of the country. No other place is more secure than Baja."

"There we are," O'Brien said. "Let's go over there."

"Well," Elizabeth said, "you have to take care of that wound first."

"Don't worry about it. The doctors at the hospital can fix me up in no time. I saw it; it's nothing more than a flesh wound. I'm not even carrying the bullet with me. But please, drive carefully."

They pulled into the hospital's emergency room entrance. The doctors and nurses tried to persuade O'Brien to get treatment for his injury, but he was firm in his insistence they move me first. Finally, he flashed his government badge. "This is a matter of national security. We need to move him to a secure place—look at what just happened to me."

Dr. Raymond reluctantly said, "OK, but keep him sedated, and he'll need to take his medicine to prevent another clot from forming for at least the next forty-eight to seventy-two hours."

A few nurses helped Zuyen and Elizabeth put me in the Navigator. A little while later, we left O'Brien at the hospital to get his wound taken care of. We reached the toll road on Highway 73.

I was lying on a stretcher in the back of the Navigator. I shook my head, opened my eyes, and said in a very soft, weak voice, "My God, what a terrible day." Even speaking was an effort.

Zuyen said, "Oh, you came back from the dead." I tried to smile, but my swollen face made even that painful.

I tried to say something, but Zuyen had to ask, "What was that, my love?"

With effort, I said, "Who is driving?" My sense of trust was profoundly shaken at this point.

Zuyen turned and looked at Elizabeth. "He just asked who's driving, Elizabeth?"

I tried to smile again, and settled for a relaxed expression. "Oh, Elizabeth. Good. Tell her hi for me."

Zuyen said, "Elizabeth, Julio Antonio says hi."

Elizabeth exclaimed, "Oh, my God! He's awake? Tell him hi back, but to go back to sleep. Tell him not to worry about anything at all, it's all under control."

Zuyen reached over and put one of my hands in hers. I drifted off to sleep, and heard my late Mima's voice speak the kind words I heard once when I was nine years old: "Sleep, my prince. You don't have anything to worry about. Tomorrow is your birthday. Maybe you will have a great surprise. Sleep, my love—sleep. Remember, you can see things before they happen. You have a great gift. Make sure you use it for good."

I opened my eyes, and Zuyen said, "Sleep, my love—sleep."

I could not see her face, however; the only face I saw was Mima's. "Don't worry about anything. It will all be OK."

I looked out one of the side windows, and watched the street lights whip by faster and faster.

Chapter 14

THE FINAL CLUE

Baja California, Mexico
Secret Location
Safe House

Front of safe house in Baja California

Elizabeth drove the Navigator, and Zuyen sat beside me. We slowed down at the border. We were well-known there, and the crossing personnel greeted us in friendly fashion. It was already very late at night. A few hours later we arrived at a multi-story house by the ocean. Elizabeth got out, opened the gate, and opened up the garage door. She parked inside, and with a great deal of difficulty, both women managed to maneuver the stretcher out of the car and carry me up to the master bedroom.

I opened my eyes and said, "I think I can help you guys."

"Shh, don't worry about it," Zuyen said. "We can handle it. Go back to sleep."

They set my stretcher down for a moment, pulled back the bedsheet, and arranged the pillows. They then shifted me from the stretcher into the bed.

Elizabeth asked Zuyen, "Do you want something to eat?"

"No, thank you. I'm stressed, and if I eat in this state I'll get an upset stomach."

"Yes, but it's not good to go without eating for so long. It's been six hours since we left Newport. Even something light." She opened a box of Ritz crackers and set them in front of Zuyen along with some peanuts and a glass of milk.

Zuyen grimaced. "OK, I'll eat a little something."

Elizabeth made herself a sandwich. They took their plates into the living room and sat down on the white leather couch by the fireplace.

"I have to thank you," Zuyen said. "You didn't just save my life, but also that of my honey. If you hadn't been around, I don't want to think about what would have happened."

Elizabeth smiled. "There's no reason to thank me for anything. Besides, it wasn't just me. The old man did a pretty good job of taking a bullet in the shoulder, but he helped put down some of those men, too. Besides, you would have done the same thing for me."

Zuyen looked at the suspended fireplace in the middle of the living room. "This is beautiful!"

Elizabeth smiled. "Our friend Julio Antonio has excellent taste, eh?"

"I can see it."

"He not only designed it, but he practically built it with the workers. You've never seen anything like it?"

"No, I've only seen a picture of it in the Caribbean island."

"'Render unto Caesar what is Caesar's.' This man has multiple talents."

Zuyen smiled once more. They could see the flames reflected against the glass of the atrium as they looked out over the ocean. They sat there a little while longer, eating their snacks.

Suspended fireplace designed by Dr. Marmol

View of the ocean from the back of the safe house

The weather the next morning was beautiful. The phone rang at around 10:00 a.m. Zuyen stretched her hand out and picked up the receiver but did not answer right away.

"This is O'Brien," said the voice on the other end. "Hello? How is everything?"

Still only half-awake, Zuyen said, "Everything is good."

"Did I wake you up? I'm sorry."

"Yeah, we got here very late last night," she replied, rubbing her eyes. "He's still groggy from the drugs. I think it will still be a few days before he can fully communicate."

"Don't forget to give him the medication for the swelling in his head," O'Brien said.

"I won't. I have it right here. How are you doing? How's your shoulder?"

"It's OK. The doctor told me it will be healed in a couple of weeks. Like I said, it's only a flesh wound. You take care of yourself as well as our man, OK?"

"You take care of yourself, too."

They hung up, and she began to change the bandage on my head. Elizabeth knocked on the door. "Come in. I'm up, I'm changing his bandage."

Elizabeth walked in with a bowl of soup. She sat it down on the love seat next to the bed. Then she rolled the office chair from my drawing table to my bedside. She sat down and began to spoon feed me the soup. I ate a little and fell back to sleep.

A few weeks later, I was feeling much better. I called out, "Zuyen! Liz, Liz!"

They both ran into the room with apprehensive expressions on their faces. I was trying to remove the bandages from my head. She looked at Elizabeth. "Get the sedatives," she said.

"Hold it," I said.

Elizabeth looked down at her arm and said, "OK, I can see you're getting your strength back, so no tranquilizer for you."

I realized I was holding Elizabeth's arm and released it. "OK, I'm sorry. I hope I didn't hurt you."

"Don't worry about it, you didn't hurt me at all." She helped me to lean back against the pillow.

"Thank you both, for everything you've done for me. I don't want any more tranquilizers, please. I want to be awake. I have a lot in my head, and I need to get it out."

"Don't worry about it," Zuyen said. "You will have plenty of time to get your payback."

Elizabeth smiled. "We have to get you back to Newport as soon as possible."

"Why?" I asked. "What is the rush?"

"We couldn't find the two CDs," she said. "We don't know where they are."

I smiled. "They should be in the Land Rover where I left them."

"Where is that?"

"Behind the license plate in the back. It should be in the CD cases for *Dare to Dream* and *In Celebration of Life*. Could someone please give me a glass of water?"

Zuyen smiled. "Sure, honey. I'll get you one."

She filled a glass and handed it to me. I took a sip. "Those CDs contain the new addresses of all the terrorists within the

United State along with plans coordinated with Castro to bring the nation to its knees. It's extremely important that O'Brien see it at once. Maybe then he'll be able to convince the high bureaucracy in the intelligence community and the politicians. They might then successfully arrest some of these people."

"How do you feel?"

"If I have to be honest, I'm still a little dizzy from these drugs. That's why I needed you stop giving me those tranquilizers. We need to figure out when and how the terrorists plan to strike. I know it will be soon and will involve airports all over the United States. They've all received pilot's training and false pilot names from Saudi Arabia. I need to put it all together if I can get my head clear."

Elizabeth said, "OK, I'll go to Newport Beach at once and talk to O'Brien." She smiled mischievously. "I'll bring him here, even if I need to tie him up. That way you can tell him everything you remember."

"OK, that would be great, honey."

"Don't worry about anything. I'll take care of it. You just sit back, enjoy the ride, and try to recuperate."

"Don't worry at all. I'll stay quiet here. But the sooner you get those CDs into O'Brien's hands, the better. That will help my recuperation a great deal. Do me a favor and bring the Land Rover back. We might need the extra car here, OK?" I reached out and touched her arm appreciatively. She smiled, patted my hand, and left to head to Newport Beach.

The next morning, Zuyen was in the kitchen preparing some fruit. I came up behind her and held her from the back. She whirled in fear, then smiled when she saw me. "You're crazy! You're getting out of bed by yourself now? I'm going to need a roll of duct tape to tie you to the bed."

I showed her my crutches. "I didn't get out by myself. I had help from these aluminum legs."

She kissed me. "You've even shaved by yourself."

We looked deeply into each other's eyes. I held her close and said, "Thank you for all the kindness you've shown me."

She smiled tenderly. "You would have done the same for me— probably even more."

We kissed again, and she felt something as I hugged her. She put her finger to her lip and said, "Ah, ah—no hanky panky or excitement. Tell your little friend to calm down. You have to rest, remember?"

I smiled. "OK. I'm very strong, but OK." I turned to get my crutches, and nearly fell over. Zuyen moved quickly to catch me. I regained my balance and my dignity.

She said, "See? I told you—you're still weak. Don't abuse your body, or you'll regret it. It will take you even longer to recover."

"Well, I'm almost fine," I amended my earlier statement.

She helped me back to the living room and we sat down at the dining table. She put some fruit in front of me, and we started to eat. At that moment, the phone rang, and I answered it.

It was Elizabeth. "I found what I was looking for in the Land Rover as you told me. I'll be there in a few days. Just relax. It's in my hands now."

"OK, honey. Thanks for your call. You've taken a great weight off my shoulders."

I hung up, and with Zuyen's assistance I walked to the hammock close to the terrace. I lay down.

A couple of days later the doorbell rang. We saw with great joy that it was Elizabeth and O'Brien. We had been on the patio barbequing when they arrived, and we all sat down around the table out there.

O'Brien said, "Oh, my God! You're barbequing already! Are you OK?"

"I'm fine," I replied. "Don't worry about it."

O'Brien smiled and said, "I'm so hungry I could eat a horse."

"Well," I answered, "you've got plenty to eat. You've got lobsters and porterhouse steaks."

Zuyen set down a large tray on the table. O'Brien took one look at it and exclaimed, "My God, were you guys expecting us? Lobster, porterhouses, and pork chops, too!"

I said, "You can eat all you want to your heart's content."

O'Brien smiled, and we all sat down to eat. "This is delicious," he said. "What did you put in this?"

Zuyen said, "It's Julio Antonio's secret recipe. You'll have to ask him."

After we finished eating, we walked out onto the balcony overlooking the ocean.

"It's not one or two guys," O'Brien said grimly. "It's twenty-one people. But we can't use the proof we have against them in a court of law. What we have won't stand up."

I smiled in frustration. "What about the illegal way?"

O'Brien raised an eyebrow. "Don't forget, outside the United States, everything is a green light. But inside the U.S., it's completely different." He took a sip of wine.

I reclined. "I understand. No one wants to take responsibility should anything go wrong. They don't want a repetition of the Zipper and the Iran-Contra Affair. All I'm asking from you is to give me the green light, and my guys will put them in a van, drive them over here, and interrogate them far away from U.S. soil. We won't hurt them, but I will guarantee you that they will talk. Even if we get nothing from any of them—which will never happen—we'll at least disrupt their internal communication and therefore their plans. Maybe we'll prevent the death of hundreds if not thousands of innocent people."

O'Brien stroked his chin. He shook his head. "For how long could you kidnap and hold these people?"

I adjusted my sunglasses and smiled. "Why did you have to use that ugly word? We'll only be holding them unharmed. We just have to hold them long enough until their plan is destroyed and they cannot kill innocent people. That's our only alternative at this moment. We know for a fact what they're going to do: kill innocent people. We don't know how they'll do it yet. We don't know where or when, but we know for sure they will do it if we cross our arms and do nothing about it."

"OK, OK, slow down," said O'Brien. "Let's assume I get the OK to do this. Where do we put these people?"

"Don't worry about it at all. The less you and your people know about this, the better. We have a very good relationship with several high-ranking authorities in this country as well as others. If we ask for their protection, they will not say no. They will facilitate us and accommodate what we're planning to do. By the way, I will assure you they will be delighted, knowing that we'll interrupt these activities."

O'Brien said, "The idea's not bad, but you're too close to us to disavow it. If it gets bad, we can't deny your existence. I will get consultation from higher authorities before I say yes or no."

"Just remember: Gaddafi in Libya, bin Laden in Sudan, and Fidel Castro in Cuba were born in the same womb and act together. We cannot be merciful. I'll call Hernesto and Yaneba so that they're ready in case we get the green light. If you give us the OK, we'll have probably a ninety percent chance to stop this. It will require time and resources and extreme confidentiality. No one, without exception, should know what we plan to do."

Elizabeth and Zuyen came over to us. Zuyen said, "Well, have you guys solved all the problems in the world?"

O'Brien half smiled. "Well, we're beginning to try. It's in process, at least. But, my young and beautiful lady, I don't think this world can be repaired. If I could have another glass of wine, that might help."

Zuyen refilled his glass. A few hours later, O'Brien and Elizabeth left the house after we exchanged hugs.

A week later, Hernesto and Yaneba were visiting me. I was off the crutches by then and we were eating and drinking Sangria on the patio. I received a call from O'Brien and took it inside.

"Those plans have received a red light," he informed me. "We will continue to try and change their minds."

I was completely frustrated by this. I returned to the patio and offered my friends coconut water with Bacardi while I expressed my frustration to them.

"Don't be mad at O'Brien," Hernesto said. "He's trying his best. It's not him or his superiors. There's a tremendous bureaucracy involved in every government, and intelligence is no exception. Remember, if something goes wrong, these politicians are afraid of losing the lucrative positions, nice meals, and comforts they have."

Yaneba smiled in frustrated irony. "It's the same thing. How will they feel if they blow up an airport or a damned plane lands on their heads?"

I raised my arms. "Wait! What did you say, Yaneba?"

She looked at me in surprise. "What do you mean?"

"What did you just say?"

"Well, maybe they'll blow up an airport."

"After that!"

"Maybe they'll land an airplane on their heads."

"That's what they're going to do!"

Hernesto and Yaneba looked at me in confusion. "What are you trying to imply?" asked Hernesto.

I said, "The 'eyes in the skies' have been watching twenty-four hours a day, and nothing like explosives has been transported anywhere. I think Yaneba just gave me the answer I've been looking for."

I stood up and hugged her, then sat back down. "I hope I'm wrong," I said with deep concern, "but even though it sounds like a crazy theory, I think these terrorists are going to steal the planes, not for sabotage or blowing up an airport."

"Steal them for what?" Yaneba asked.

"They've received training to fly the planes, but what's the purpose in that? They must be using the planes as weapons! They can hit the Golden Gate Bridge or something."

Yaneba slammed back the coconut drink and shook her head. "The last kamikazes were in World War II, if I remember. I cannot believe somebody would be so stupid as to kill himself. For what?"

"Remember, these people are extremists. They might not care about living or dying. Or they might have put a couple of parachutes in each plane. As soon as they fly the plane low enough, they could jump from it. For money, people are capable of doing anything, and for enough money, maybe someone could close their eyes and put a couple parachutes on the plane. It's not even illegal. They could carry parachutes or even a glide suit in a travel bag."

We all looked at each other. Hernesto and Yaneba began to realize the idea wasn't that crazy. I shook my head. "It's actually a brilliant idea. Horrible, but brilliant. And you actually gave me it, Yaneba. Was that what you were thinking when you said that?"

She shook her head. "No, I was thinking they would sabotage the planes so they would crash later."

We all stayed silent for several minutes. Zuyen shook her head nervously. She then said something prophetic: "Can you imagine what they could do with a Boeing 747 with all that gas on board?"

I shook my head. "Oh, my God! It's been four months since I came back from Cuba. I have a strong conviction something big will happen—not from my rational mind but a gut feeling. All of these people going through so much intensive training…."

I rushed over and snatched the phone. I called O'Brien's number, but there was no answer.

I called Elizabeth. As soon as she picked up, I said, "Honey, get ahold of O'Brien at once! I think I've figured out what exactly they are going to do, but I don't want to say over the phone. Remember that we've got the red light, and I don't want to be accused of overreacting. This might change in the next hour or the next day. Please let him know that I need to see him in person. Thank you." I hung up the phone and turned to the others.

Everyone looked at each other in shock. Later that evening, Hernesto and Yaneba left to return to the United States. I watched them leave, and said to Zuyen, "My God! No wonder those cowardly criminals in Cuba keep saying they'll bring the U.S to its knees. Let's hope they don't crash one of these planes into the White House."

Zuyen said, "Let's hope you're wrong."

I replied, "I would love to be wrong."

Preventative Medicine for Hope and Change

In deep concern I dug through my brain, trying to discover before it's too late the remedy and the way to prevent from ever happening again the possibility of any political leader to bring tears to the eyes of our people. With their deceitful veil, they prevent people from seeing them for what they are and take away by force our freedom and betray our laws forever by changing the way we live our lives.

As we look into the sky and see the storm which is coming, obviously the sky is dark and the sun doesn't shine; in the same way, we should take the time to educate our people and open their eyes. We should not believe a false prophet or the rhetoric of a politician, because there's never hope and change unless one has an intelligent, educated mind. When you're thirsty and frustrated, let us not forget that the ocean only can provide you with salt water, even though it appears crystal clear and good to drink. You live on the river with good, sweet water at your feet. It is truly ironic for you to be unable to appreciate and value what we always have.

Dr. Julio Antonio del Mármol

Chapter 15

A PROFOUND LACK OF JUDGMENT

Sept. 10, 2001

Since it was the off-season, we had the whole beach to ourselves. There wasn't a soul around, just the birds and the ocean. We had spent the day very harmoniously, walking the beach, lying under the umbrella, eating an excellent chicken fricassee I had taught Zuyen to make, and drinking a bottle of wine. We watched the sun set behind the mountains. Faint shadows were cast by the dim light of the crescent moon.

The romance of the setting, combined with the harmony with which we had enjoyed that day, made both of us amorous. Covered by the blankets, we made tender, beautiful love. By about 9:00 it was starting to get chilly, so we decided it was time to return to the house.

We took a hot Jacuzzi bath to wash the salt water from our bodies before bedtime. We turned on a small television set that sat on a pedestal located in the bathroom and watched the international news. When we finished our bath, we dried off and went to the kitchen to make a late dessert. It was by now 10:45 p.m.

I opened a can of mangoes. I added some vanilla ice cream and baptized the fruit with Grand Marnier. We took our dessert up to the bedroom on a small tray and indulged ourselves. I grew tired and was about to remove the tray from the bed, but Zuyen stopped me.

"No, sweetie, let me take it to the kitchen," she said.

"Thank you," I said. Shortly after that, I fell into a deep sleep.

I began to sweat profusely, and I woke to my own voice screaming, "No, no! For God's sake, there are women and children there!" As I turned over, I felt my hand make impact with something. I opened my eyes and saw that my hand had flopped onto Zuyen's face quite hard. She cried out in pain and rolled off the bed, her head hitting the marble floor.

"Those cowards!" I yelled, still half-asleep.

I sat up in bed, and looked at Zuyen as she stood up from the floor. I immediately noticed the bump on her head. She could tell from my continued loud, incoherent shouting that I was still partially asleep, deep in whatever nightmare was disturbing me. She went quickly to the minibar refrigerator by the bed and took out a bottle of cold water. She ran back to me and began to splash me in the face with it.

I shook my head in bemusement. "Who are you? What are you doing?" I exclaimed.

She said, "Love, you're having a nightmare. It's me!"

I covered my face with my hands, partly to wipe away the water but also to shake my head. I looked back up at her and said in a very calm voice, "What happened to your eye?" She turned to look at the long mirror on the wall, and saw the large swollen bump above her eye. I asked again in a concerned voice, "What happened?"

She said soothingly, "You hit me. I tried to wake you up, and you knocked me out of the bed. When I fell, I hit my head on the floor."

I jumped out of bed like I had been shocked. I put my arms around her. "I'm sorry, honey, I'm sorry." As I walked her to the bathroom, I asked, "How did this happen?"

She smiled, half-jokingly, "You'd better put a patch on my eye quickly, or the people who see me tomorrow will think you're a wife beater."

While she teased me, I examined the bump. "How could I have done that much damage? You have a small cut there."

"I told you, when you hit me, I fell onto the floor. That cut came from hitting my head against the marble."

I shook my head, got on my knees before her, and kissed her hands. "I'm sorry, honey, I'm sorry."

"Stop it," she chided gently. "You'll make me feel terrible. You've already told me about your dreams. It wasn't you—you didn't know what you were doing." She caressed my head as I knelt before her. "Poor Julio Antonio. You must have had a terrible nightmare. You were screaming so loudly. I tried to wake you up, and you had tears in your eyes, like you were crying. What were you dreaming?"

I replied, "You have no idea how bad that dream was. I saw four or five planes simultaneously hitting a very tall building. There were women and children inside. I saw those same people, all ages, jumping to the street below rather than be burned by the fire." I put both hands to my head.

She shook her head. "Don't worry. It's only a bad dream."

"You know what my nightmares represent. They're premonitions of what will happen in a very short time."

She shook her head again. "No, it won't be like that, not this time. Let's go back to bed now."

"No," I said. "You go back to bed. I'm going to wash my face. I don't want to sleep anymore."

Zuyen noticed something beneath my pajamas. "What is that?"

There were scratches all over my chest, as if done by fingernails. She checked my nails and hers to see if there was any flesh or blood beneath them, but they were clean. She checked the bed to see what could have made the marks but found nothing.

"How in God's name did that happen to you?" she exclaimed, deeply disturbed.

She took a cotton ball and began to clean the deep scratches with antiseptic. When she finished, she brought me a glass of orange juice and one of my tranquilizers. I waved them off. "No, I want to call O'Brien."

"At this time of night? It's so late—it's almost one a.m. on the East Coast."

"I don't care." As she dressed, I dialed the number of his private line.

His voice when he answered was surprised and concerned. "What's happened?" he asked.

"I'm sorry to call you this late, my friend, but I'm coming back tonight. Right now."

"No! Wait—it's not safe for you here. I didn't want to tell you before, but—your friend from Gelson's seafood market, John—did you give anything to him?"

"No, why?"

"Are you sure? Just remember. Think back."

"Oh, yeah—he's got one of my pistols, the one I was carrying that day. He also had the decoy disk in a magnetic box."

"I'm sorry to tell you, my friend, he and his family are all dead. They were all found shot in their house."

"What? Are you sure?"

"Absolutely sure. That's why I'm telling you not to cross the border. You're safe there. Please, don't come here until we can apprehend these people and put them in a restricted area. Remember, we don't know where those people who attacked you are. We're investigating. Evidently one of them saw you give John something, and that cost him his life and the lives of his family."

"I'm very sorry to hear that, but I'm coming anyway," I said firmly. "I'm already dressed, and I'll be heading towards the border in a bit."

"I guess you won't take no for an answer. In that case, be very careful, and don't let a single soul know you're coming this way. Do you intend to leave Zuyen there?"

"No. I will bring her with me. Don't worry—I'll be cautious." Zuyen had heard the entire conversation. I turned around and said, "We have to go."

She looked at me in concern. "I don't think you care for your life or mine, for that matter. Why do you want to go back there? This is crazy!"

I said, "If you want, you can stay here. I'll only be there for a day or two."

There were tears in Zuyen's eyes. "Will you please at least wait until morning, and not leave at this crazy hour?"

"I'm sorry, honey, but I have to go now."

As she put her ice bag down, I could see she was crying. I put my arm around her shoulder, but she waved me off. "I don't want to stay here alone."

"No," I agreed. "I think you should go immediately to Mexico City to your father and wait for me there until I come back. I think you'll be more secure there."

"No," she said stubbornly, "I'm going with you."

"I don't think it's safe for you there."

"Remember what you said: anywhere you go, I go."

I knew when it was time to give in. "OK. Get dressed."

She quickly dressed, and we got into the Land Rover. A couple of hours later we were driving through the Mexican desert in silence. I still felt bad about her eye, and she thought I was behaving irrationally. We soon entered the city of Mexicali and came to a roundabout with five avenues merging across two railroad tracks. I saw a train coming and stopped before crossing the tracks.

A large car stopped behind me, an olive sedan with two men inside. The car looked somehow familiar, and they stopped far too close for my comfort. I could see that there were trains coming from either direction. Even though it was by now 3:00 a.m., people were out buying tacos from a stand nearby. Both trains blew their whistles as they approached the crossing, and the sedan suddenly rammed us.

I stomped hard on the brake, but the powerful car behind us started to move us onto the crossing. Zuyen yelled, "What are these people doing?"

I realized that we couldn't get out of the Land Rover, so I activated the four-wheel drive, jammed the gearshift into reverse, and released the clutch even as I pressed hard on the gas pedal. The Land Rover jumped back, forcing the sedan backwards. The grill of our car, however, would still get clipped by the train. Zuyen's eyes bulged in terror as she saw sparks flying outside the window even as the smell of burning rubber wafted through the air. She screamed in utter panic as she clung to the internal bars for her very life.

We struggled to get clear by pushing the sedan back onto the other set of railroad tracks. They started to get out of their car. Seeing that, I let go of the accelerator to allow them to get their car clear of the track, making them decide to stay with their vehicle. Then I stomped hard on the accelerator, shoving them half-way onto the track.

The two men ran from their car, the first one pulling a gun as he did so. I put the Land Rover into gear and drove off the track. The other two men tried to run—but it was too late, and they were hit by the train. By the powerful light of the engine, however, I could see their faces clearly. They were the same men who attacked me in Gelson's Market.

A piece of metal flew from the rear of their car and cut the Land Rover's soft top, about a nine-inch-long tear.

I drove quickly away, maneuvering around the scrap metal. I took Zuyen's hand and asked, "You OK, sweetie?"

She nodded nervously. "Yes—but I have to use the restroom. You understand, don't you?"

I smiled. "Yes, honey—I understand."

I drove until I reached the Hotel Lucerna, and pulled over there. I greeted a couple of the people who worked there that knew me, letting them know that we were just stopping to use the restrooms on our way through. She went immediately to the women's restroom, and from inside I could hear the sounds of her vomiting.

I went into the men's room and balanced my briefcase on the sink counter. As I pulled my telephone out, it slipped from my hand and fell into the sink. It began to make a strange buzzing noise. I picked it up and opened the battery compartment. I was surprised to discover a chip next to the battery. I removed the chip before calling O'Brien. "Hello?" he asked. "How are you doing? Are you back already?"

"No, I haven't crossed the border yet, but I'm close," I said. "I wanted to tell you that someone just tried to kill us before we reached it."

I yanked the receiver away from my ear as he exploded. I could still hear his voice clearly. "I *told* you not to come!"

"Calm down," I replied, "we are OK. The great news is that the rest of the guys who tried to kill me at Gelson's are dead. This doesn't concern me; what does concern me is that I just found a tracking device on my phone. This is the reason I'm calling you now. Who was handling my phone while I was unconscious?"

"It could have been anyone," he said. "While you were unconscious, they found it in the ambulance. It could have been one of the ambulance attendants."

"Yes," I answered, "it could also have been one of your guys, as well. Zuyen told me that one of your personal security men handed that phone to her."

"Yes, that's right. And one of them almost killed me, too. We never know who we've got around until a situation like that comes up. There's nothing you or I can do. It's the business we've chosen to be in."

"OK," I said. "Let's change the location. We're not going to be in the Hilton by the airport. Let's go to the Number Two location."

O'Brien asked, "The last Number Two or the earlier Number Two?"

"The earlier one," I said. We hung up and I met Zuyen in the lobby. We walked out to the Land Rover together. Once inside the vehicle, I showed her the chip.

"What is that?" she asked.

"This chip is how our enemies tracked us down. Somebody put it in my cell phone."

"I knew it! That gorilla must have done it."

I looked at her in surprise. "You know who did this?"

"You remember what I told you about one of O'Brien's guys, what he did while you were unconscious? He almost ran us off the road because he was so busy trying to look under my skirt? I knew that man had to be more than merely unclassy and vulgar. He had to be one of our enemies. He was the one who drove us home from the hospital." She took the chip between her fingers and shook her head as she examined it.

I shook my head as well. "No wonder. I always say, never expect loyalty from those you pay, because someone can always come along and pay them more than you. Let's go."

I started the engine and we left the hotel parking lot. She asked, "What do I do with this?"

"Throw it away."

She rolled down the window and tossed it out into the street.

"How do you feel?" I asked.

"I feel better. I threw up all my food from last night. It had apparently been stuck there following the beating I got from you in the middle of the night along with the stress of having to return to the United States in the early morning hours. The last straw was the fireworks we had on the railroad tracks."

I smiled. "Do you want to eat something before we cross the border?"

"No, water is all I need. I'm thirsty, and my mouth is dry."

I reached behind me and pulled a bottle of water out of the cooler behind me. I handed it to her. I reached into one of my compartments and found a plastic cup. "Reach into the glove compartment, and you'll find some Alka-Seltzer. Drop a couple of those in a half-cup of water, and you'll feel better."

She watched the bubbling concoction for a second. She drank it down thirstily and burped a few times. "Oops. I'm sorry," she excused herself.

"That's OK." I patted her on the back. "Feel better?"

"Yes, a lot. Thank you."

"Now you need to eat something and relax."

Border Crossing at Mexicali

We were approaching the border. It was so early in the morning that there were only two cars in line ahead of us. We moved forward after they received the green light from border security.

The guard approached us. "Identification, please. What nationality are you?"

There was something about him that raised my guard. He seemed to be some kind of Asian mix, but predominately white with dark curly hair, green eyes, approximately in his 40s. Something in the way he spoke made me feel uncomfortable.

Zuyen said as she handed him her passport, "I am an American citizen."

"What about you, sir?"

"Technically, I'm an American as well."

He looked at my green card. "But it says here you're Cuban."

I looked over my glasses at him. "But where is Cuba? In Asia? In Europe? It's in America. That makes me an American."

He didn't take the joke very well and frowned. "Well, you're still a Cuban."

"And I'm proud of it as well as being an American. I've been here in the United States, in *North* America, for about thirty years. How about you? What nationality are you?"

The guard couldn't hold it back any more and smiled. "What?" he said, taken aback.

"You have an accent, and you look Asian. You definitely don't belong here, unlike me."

The guard shook his head and said, "You're right. I'm from Haiti. And you're also right—you've been here longer than me. I've been here ten years." He was relaxed by now. "You should be proud to be Cuban, man. You guys are famous around the world. Scarface." He made a gun shape with his hand. "My little friend," he said. My green card still in his hand, he punched some numbers into the terminal. He grew pale.

The gates suddenly closed as sirens went off. He backed hastily away. "Don't move, don't move!" He fumbled for the gun at his waist, struggling to get it clear.

I raised my arms. "I'm not armed. I'm getting out."

Zuyen was completely freaking out at this point. More guards ran out, ordering me out of the car. She screamed, "You don't know how he is? He works with the government in intelligence!"

I said to her, "Shh. It's OK, honey. Calm down. I'll take care of this."

They trained M-16 rifles on me as two other guards moved in to arrest me. Zuyen shook her head as if to say, "Not again." One guard got in the driver's seat and drove it over to the inspection area. She was asked to leave the car as they searched it. They threw contents all over the place, making an absolute mess of the interior of my Land Rover, while Zuyen watched silently.

At the same time, they walked me into one of the small cells in the building and strip searched me. One of the guards shoved me into position for the search. I said to him, "I will do whatever you want. There's no need to be a jerk. I'm not resisting, and will cooperate to the fullest. When you've finished with all this bullshit, all I want to know is the reason for all of this."

The Haitian guard said, "I'm sorry. The only thing I can tell you is what the computer told us: you're armed and dangerous. Our supervisor can give you more details." He had a little more confidence and sympathy for me, and asked, "Has anyone been using your ID?"

I looked him straight in the eye. "Man, I've lost my sense of humor. I don't know if you're joking or if this is another bad dream like I had this morning before I headed this way. How the hell am I going to know if anyone used my ID or not?"

They took their sweet time to check every stitch of my clothes, while I stood there in the cell stark naked, wearing only my underwear. The Haitian guard asked me to remove it, as well. One of the guards was female, so I asked, "Would you please have the lady leave, so that I can remove it and keep at least some dignity, man?"

She said condescendingly, "Honey, I've seen it *all*!"

The Haitian guard intervened. "Maria, would you please step into the other room?"

After they finished, finding me absolutely clean, I was told to get dressed. The Haitian guard said, "Our supervisor wants to speak with you in private."

I got dressed and was taken to an office. The man introduced himself as Joseph. "I'm the supervisor on this shift. I want to apologize for what just happened."

"Not a problem. I know this kind of things happen. Nice to meet you, Joseph. But really, I need to know the real reason for this, not the stupid excuse I was given. Who put this in the computer? I know how these things work. Someone put that in there intentionally to slow me down. Maybe that's above your clearance, but it's extremely important to know who is responsible for it, for my own security as well as the lady that's driving with me in the car."

Joseph stood up and walked around his desk, placing his hand on my shoulder. In an apologetic tone, he said, "I can only tell you what my bosses told me. We don't like to do this to people. According to what I know, the Secret Service put this warrant on you twelve years ago for making counterfeit currency in Los Angeles."

I smiled and shook my head. "With all my respect, Joseph, what you've been told is bullshit. Would you like to know now many times I've crossed this border since 1989? Thousands of times. This has never happened before. Go back out there and tell your bosses to come up with a better excuse. I'm not going to leave until I have a satisfactory answer."

"OK, let me see what I can do. You can go out there and wait with the lady." He walked me out of the building and over to Zuyen.

I was extremely upset by this time, but my anger increased when I saw the mess they had made of our luggage and the interior of my car. There was also some damage—the handle on one of the suitcases had been broken, and the zipper on the back cover of the jeep was also broken.

I said, "This was completely unnecessary. What the hell is this?" He shook his head. "I'm sorry, Dr. Mármol." He knelt down and helped me pick things up. "I'm going to chew someone's ass for this. They should have put everything back the way they found it."

He pulled out a pad and tore off a slip, which he handed to me. "If you find anything damaged or have any complaints, please fill out this form. Whoever conducted this search not only violated procedure but also crossed the line in the sloppy way they handled your stuff."

I took the form from him and handed it over to Zuyen. Joseph continued, "I don't think this guy knows we have enough enemies in the world that we don't have to make more by acting this way."

I knew it wasn't his fault, but I wanted to put more pressure on him. "Don't worry about it. It's not about the luggage. Like I told you before, I want in writing the reason I was pulled over and disturbed in this way. I'm not going to leave here until I get that. Go back and tell your boss that."

"OK, let me see what I can do." He walked back into the building. Forty-five minutes passed, and I was growing very agitated.

Finally, he came back out, bearing a very long face. He held out one of his personal cards. "If you need me as a witness for what happened here today, you can use me. This is completely off the record, what I'm going to say now. My boss said that this is completely out of his hands. He has no idea why that was in the computer. He's been on the phone all this time, and he hasn't been given a straight answer. They just kept transferring him from one department to another. You could stay here for weeks, but you won't get a direct answer. You're going to have to go above our level to find out what happened here." He held out his hand to me. "I'm sorry again."

"I'll get to the bottom of this. Thank you for your effort." I shook his hand and said goodbye. I could see that Zuyen was ecstatic to drive away from that place.

Reply Dr. Marmol received from CBP. The burn damage is the result of the document being inside a car that was bombed in an attempt on Dr. Marmol's life.

U.S. Customs and Border Protection

1300 PENNSYLVANIA AVENUE, NW &c
WASHINGTON, DC 20229

OFFICIAL BUSINESS
PENALTY FOR PRIVATE USE $300

Accompanying envelope, also damaged in the bombing attempt.

Dr. Julio A. Marmol Barrios
427 East 17th Street Apt. 232
Costa Mesa, CA 92627

Phone:
Fax:

US Customs & Border Protection
F.O.I.A. - CSU
Room 5.5C
1300 Pennsylvania Ave. N.W.
Washington, DC 20229

Phone: 877-CBP-5511

Date:

RE: Incident in Calexico/Mexicaly Boarder

Dear Sirs:

This early morning, returning from Baja California, the boarder patrol slide my "Permanent Resident Card" (INS A# 018-827-638 issued 27 September 1971) and for ████████████ I was handcuffed at my car and escorted at gun-point by approximately ten boarder guards to the inside premises.

I was ordered to strip, bodily searched, and put into a small cell.

This was a great embarrassment to me ████████████ and was just as rude the second time this happened, today, especially since the supervisor named Joseph, apologized to me the ██ time, saying t h a t t h e c o m p u t e r s a i d t h a t I w a s : "armed and dangerous" and that he would report this to his superior, as this situation could develop into a fatal accident (mine) by this computer mistake.

No mater that there was damage done to my car during this ██ incident; I did NOT file the complaint form that Joseph gave me, wishing to get this despicable event behind me.

Since this has happened ███ and this derogatory and fallacious remark is STILL in the computer TODAY shows me that Joseph, indeed, did not attend to it or that he did not have the authority to handle this matter.

I implore you to please get to the bottom of this situation as soon as possible and correct this mistake because I'm NOT "armed" and far from "dangerous."

I cross this boarder at lease once a month. I don't have a record of violence.

I am the ████████████████████████████████

Any assistance in telling me how this situation came about, I would greatly appreciate knowing as this might help me prevent this absudity in the future.

I am aware of today's volatile situations at our boarders, and appreciate knowing all the care your agency is giving to protect against another 911-attack; but, it is just this same volatility that alarms me and prompts me to have this correction-of-fact corrected, so that I do not become an innocent victim of this volatility.

I eagerly await the results of you investigation into this computer description as "armed and dangerous" and have it removed, as it is fallacious and misleading.

Respectfully yours,

Dr. Julio A. Marmol Barrios. PhD

California, DL # N 079 49 21. Expires 5/28

EDGAR DE LA TORRE
Commission # 1486492
Notary Public - California
Orange County
My Comm. Expires May 25, 2008

Letter of protest to Customs and Border
Protection regarding his treatment

We drove another four hours and entered the city of Costa Mesa. We drove to the Red Lion Inn, went up to the penthouse, and took a shower together. Zuyen caressed the scratches on my chest, giving each one a tender kiss. We embraced, and she grew emotional.

Costa Mesa Hilton Hotel, formerly the Red Lion Inn

She said, "My God—what you've been telling me. I'm scared, because you told me about this happening in your childhood, and that it's repeated a couple of times since then. If these scratches happen just before something really bad happens, what could be coming now?"

I also was worried, and in a voice thick with emotion, I replied, "I know. The only things that scare me are those things without any logical explanation. I should never have told you these intimate details of my life. This not only happened in my childhood, but has happened all my life growing up, teenage years into adulthood, without fail."

The water ran over both of us as we spoke. Our shower done, we got out. Zuyen said, "I'm sorry, my love."

"I'm the one who should be sorry. Look at that eye, look at what happened to you. I feel very responsible for it."

"Don't feel that way. I can tell it wasn't your fault. You were asleep, in another state."

September 11, 2001

The hotel phone rang. I answered it, and O'Brien said, "I'm sorry I'm late. I'm in the lobby."

"Don't worry. You're just in time. We just got out of the shower. We'll be ready in a few minutes. Come on up."

O'Brien came up to the penthouse, and the three of us started to have breakfast.

The telephone rang again. I answered, and Elizabeth said, "You're not going to believe this. As you asked, we've been following all of the subjects. Are ready? I'll read to you our report and conclusions regarding their flight itinerary. A first group of subjects boarded American Airlines Flight 11, a Boeing 767 with ninety-two people. They departed Logan Airport in Boston at 7:59 am Eastern Daylight Time, bound for Los Angeles International Airport. At 8:14, a second group of subjects boarded United Airlines Flight 175, another Boeing 767. They departed Logan, this one with sixty-five people on board. It was also bound for Los Angeles International." Elizabeth finished by telling me, "Two or three of our subjects are in place on each on these planes."

I shook my head in clear disgust and said, "Oh, my God. This is happening the way we thought it would. Please keep me posted." We said goodbye and hung up.

I looked at O'Brien and said, "I think we're a little too late. They're in motion." By that time, O'Brien, Zuyen, and I had almost finished our breakfast in the penthouse.

Zuyen explained what had happened to us at the border. O'Brien was taken completely by surprise. Even he found it hard to believe the extremes these men were willing to go to. He shook his head. "I told Julio Antonio to not cross the border unless we caught his attackers first."

"I knew the tall guy with the green eyes," I said. "I cannot understand how anybody managed to turn him against us. This guy had been with you for a long time."

O'Brien replied, "You know by now that, without exception, anyone poses a threat of turning against us. This is especially true when an enormous amount of money is circulating, and you become so dangerous they will pay any amount to get rid of you. By now, they probably won't rest until they put you out of business."

I said, "Did Elizabeth debrief you and explain what I think these people are planning? She just confirmed to me that my nightmare will become a horrible reality at any moment."

O'Brien nodded. "Yes. Several days ago. I passed that information along, and they've been working on it—but not fast enough. I recommended the highest measures of security possible. In fact, we've even changed the president's itinerary. Not just based on the information you provided to us; your hunch itself was enough to warrant it. We've moved him to a strategic point and will keep him far away from the spots we think are the greatest risk over the next month."

"I was expecting something better than that." I shook my head, adding drily, "Well, at least we've got one person protected."

I leaned back. "It could be weeks from now. It could be hours. I'm convinced of that now, more than ever." I touched the scratches on my chest. "I only hope I'm wrong."

I continually checked my watches. I felt these responses from the White House were a little weak, but I knew why no stronger action was possible. There simply wasn't sufficient evidence. As I had frequently observed to O'Brien, the United States' greatest strength was the freedom she afforded those who walked about inside her. It was also her greatest weakness, as our enemies could walk about unrestrained, provided they were careful not to arouse suspicion by acting too overtly.

It was by now 8:20 a.m. Elizabeth called again and said, "We have more of our subjects in the air. From Dulles Airport, American Airlines Flight 77, a Boeing 757 departed Washington for Los Angeles International Airport with sixty-four people on board."

"Is there nothing you can do to arrest these people?" Zuyen asked.

I smiled and shook my head silently. O'Brien replied, "Believe me, Zuyen, we've been pushing every single button, looking for any reason. But we have to have something tangible in our hands in order to obtain an arrest warrant."

Zuyen, O'Brien, and I sat down in the living room to continue our conversation, and the phone rang. I answered and heard Elizabeth exclaim, "Man, man, man! All the targets are on the move. Each of them is on a different plane. They all got past the metal detectors—evidently, they're clean. They're all going to Los Angeles. This has to be an extremely coordinated plan. I have no doubt in my mind any more. Are you and Zuyen OK?"

"Yes, we're fine," I said. "Are you guys OK?"

"So far," she answered.

O'Brien looked at me grimly, seeing my face as I hung up the phone. I was feeling a little panicked, and he had never seen me that way before. I took a long, deep breath before speaking. "Elizabeth just informed me that all of these terrorists are on different airplanes bound for Los Angeles."

He stroked his forehead with his left fingers.

I said, "I think we're a little too late to stop whatever these guys are doing. It's already in motion."

O'Brien blew up. "For God's sake, don't be so pessimistic! You've never been a pessimist. Maybe they're changing their plans because they know we're breathing down their necks. Maybe they're flying to LAX to head to Mexico and are in retreat." I made no reply, but I threw him a dirty look. "What? We have to be optimistic."

This time I replied, "I don't think what you just said you even believe yourself. I hope you're right and that is the case, my friend. But I'm very unhappy about how this has been handled since the beginning. It's been months since I sent you guys this information from Mexico—a long time ago, after that attempt to kill me in the airport in Mexico City. What has been done? Practically nothing." I poured myself a glass of water and checked one of my watches. It was 8:42 a.m. on the East Coast, and Elizabeth called again to inform me that another group of subjects was boarding United Airlines Flight 93, a Boeing 757 carrying forty-four people. It departed Newark International Airport, this time bound for San Francisco.

O'Brien's phone rang. "Hello? Yes. OK, keep me informed." He hung up and looked at me, concern all over his face. There was no trace of optimism left. "That was Addison. He received information from the North American Aerospace Defense Command. There are suspected hijackers on American Flight 11. It was called in at 8:32. NORAD's scrambling two F-15s from Otis National Air Guard Base."

I stretched my legs out before me as I leaned back in my chair. I covered my face with both hands. "Oh, shit. Oh, shit. I can't believe it."

The hotel phone next to me rang again. I picked it up, and it was Elizabeth again. "What's up?" I asked.

"Sergeant went on United Airlines Flight 93. Hernesto followed him onto the plane. There's no doubt something big is in motion. We've been monitoring him, and Hernesto bought a ticket previously to see if he could find out what is up." Suddenly, she gasped in shock.

"What!?" I exclaimed anxiously.

"Do you have a TV? Turn it on."

I jumped up and turned the TV on, ignoring O'Brien's exclaimed questions. The North Tower of the World Trade Center was on fire. Elizabeth's voice on the phone yelled, "I told these stupid people! God damn it!"

We all three stood in shock, staring at the TV. At that moment, we saw a plane fly directly into the South Tower. Zuyen screamed and began to weep. She said, "I can't take this anymore."

We could see people jumping from the windows, exactly as I had seen in my nightmare. I looked at O'Brien, and he looked at me. Both of us were completely shocked, and O'Brien had tears in his eyes. He said, "You should get out of the country, right now. If not for yourself, then for her. There's nothing else you can do here now. Go."

I shook my head. I said to Zuyen, "Let's go." I turned back to O'Brien. "Yes, we're going to leave. I'm going to take her as far away from all this shit as I can. I will disappear for a while. I need to take some time off to recoup from my frustration over all the stupidity I've been watching so far developing right before my eyes."

We went down to the lobby and embraced before parting. O'Brien got in his car, and I went down to the underground garage. Zuyen and I got into the Land Rover, and the two vehicles left, heading in different directions.

Just before we reached the 405 freeway, we saw a small group of people with anti-war signs reading, "We Brought This on Ourselves" and "USA, Take Your Hands off the Rest of the World, We Should Be Ashamed."

I was very upset at the sight of the protestors, and pulled over to the side. I got out, and Zuyen yelled at me, "What are you doing? Remember, these people are ignorant, but they're also innocent!"

I didn't listen, but continued to approach them with my pistol in my hand. Zuyen continued to yell after me to stop, trying to remind me that these people had absolutely nothing to do with what had just happened.

As soon as they saw me and the   deranged expression on my face, they fearfully dropped their signs and started to run off. I shook my head in disgust as I came to my senses. What Zuyen had said was true, and I had to ask myself what I was going to do—shoot them? I was the one out of line, the one overreacting. I turned and headed back to the Land Rover.

I opened the door and climbed back in. I looked into Zuyen's eyes. "I'm sorry, honey—I lost it for a moment. Because of the ignorance and stupidity of a few today, hundreds or thousands of innocent people have been lost in the most horrible way, being burned alive in those buildings or leaping to their deaths. It's simply not fair, the deaths of these innocent people in the eyes of God or anyone."

***I-405 Freeway on ramp where
protesters gathered***

I heard on the radio at 9:21 a.m. that all the bridges and tunnels into Manhattan had been closed. By 9:37, we were well on our way to San Diego, and we heard that American Flight 77 had crashed into the west side of the Pentagon. Then at 9:42 the FAA had shut down all airports nationwide, ordering all flights grounded. At 9:45, Flight 93 flew back, and they received confirmation that they were going to fight the terrorists that were hijacking the flight. At 9:59, we heard that the South Tower had collapsed, and we continued on our way to the border. At 10:03, United 93 crashed near Shanksville, Pennsylvania.

We looked at each other in complete silence.

I pulled over in the middle of nowhere. I got out of the Land Rover and walked some distance away, Zuyen following me to see what was wrong. I put my hands to my face, shaking my head slowly from side to side. "Hernesto," I moaned, "Hernesto—oh, my God! Hernesto was on that flight."

Zuyen looked at me tearfully in emotional pain, embraced me, and we both wept. Distressed at the terrible moment, we walked over to a large rock by the highway with tears in our eyes. There we mourned the certain death of our friend who had been on that flight. We knew full well that his noble and brave character had motivated him to attempt to prevent those terrorists from reaching their goal. We knew for certain that he had given his life in that attempt.

After a while, we pulled ourselves back together and returned to the Land Rover. We got in and drove off, continuing our journey in silence. We both imagined what might have occurred inside that plane before it crashed.

At 10:10 a.m., some of the Pentagon walls collapsed. At 10:28, the North Tower collapsed. At 10:45, President George W. Bush landed at Barksdale Air Force Base. At 11:04, we heard that the United Nations had been evacuated. The radio carried President Bush's brief two-minute address to the nation at 11:36. At 12:04 p.m., LAX was closed and evacuated. At 12:15, San Francisco Airport was closed and evacuated as we crossed the border into Mexico.

I stopped in Tijuana, went into a bank, and exchanged my passports. I returned to the jeep and gave Zuyen another passport. I said, "Put your real passport somewhere no one will find it. I suggest you put it in your underwear." After she changed her passport, we drove to an isolated location where we were picked up by a waiting helicopter with Elizabeth inside and Chopin piloting.

Elizabeth stepped out to greet us. She took one look at my depressed expression and said, "Hey, don't blame yourself. You did everything humanly possible to prevent this. Sometimes we win, sometimes we lose, but don't blame yourself for it. There is a difference between us and them: we have rules we have to follow, and they don't."

I nodded. "I'm not blaming us or anyone in the intelligence community for this. We had our hands tied. I'm extremely angry, and if I have to blame anyone it is the lack of judgment of the politicians and the bureaucrats that did not act quickly enough on our intelligence, leaving open this big window of opportunity for our enemies to commit this horrible crime."

We got seated in the helicopter, and I stared out the window as we lifted off. We flew off into the sky and disappeared over the horizon.

This ends Part 1 of *ISIS: the Genetic Conception.* The master spy's mission is far from over as he continues his fight against Cuban-backed Muslim extremists as they morph into an even greater global threat in Part 2 of *ISIS: the Genetic Conception, The Shackles on Our Democracy.*

The Joy of Life

The joy in living is to live day by day and be thankful for every breath of air you take. It is being happy with yourself, no matter what situation you are in.

Even if the new day doesn't bring all you want, accept it because maybe that next day can be the best of the days in your life.

Only through optimism and with happiness in your heart can you go through life looking at the trees, on the oceans, and to the sky, and thank God because you are able to see them and are still alive to enjoy them.

I'm walking in the rain with no cover over my head. Others look at me in surprised astonishment. Nothing really is strange; I just enjoy the rain on my face as another gift of life.

In another simple thing in life is not to be afraid, whether of water on your face or anything else. Never allow anyone or anything, especially another man, to take your God, your freedom, and the things you most love in your life.

Dr. Julio Antonio del Mármol

A NOTE FROM THE AUTHOR TO THE READER

I am a man with a passionate love for the truth. I was asked by my editor today to change the word "Massa" because it might be offensive, considered racist, or not be politically correct. With all my love and respect, I said no. I know it was in her best intention to protect my image and get the best product before the eyes of the public. I have to thank her, because her suggestion not only displayed a noble intention on her part, but also because she inspired me to write this note today.

The word "Massa" as used in this book by that great black man and one of my best friends and freedom fighters, Chopin, is the one he himself used. It is worth clarifying, for the record, with courage that not only this word but others that could be and are considered even worse ones: "nigger," "slave in chains," and "son of a whore" are used daily in countries all over Hispanic America as well as in other countries in the world. Between friends, as outrageous as it may sound, these can even be affectionately meant. We use among ourselves in North America such words which can have negative connotations like "crazy," "dumb bell," "slave driver," or "Indian chief." These aren't necessarily used with the intention of giving offense or displaying racism. I always say that it's not the word used which can be offensive; it is the intention of the individual using such words.

Sometimes, the real ill intent comes from those who try to divide and silence us make us afraid and force us to avoid using certain words out of a reluctance to be accused of being racist, offensive, or politically incorrect. It is the beginning not only of closing the mouth and one's mind to the truth, but also that of the complete extermination of one's freedom of expression. Those who make these rules enforce them through intimidation. In letting yourself be so intimidated, you are converted into a regular sheep.

From my point of view, no word should ever be classified as offensive, save for those words which express obscenity or gross vulgarity. Even so, we should take into consideration the nature of the person who intentionally uses such words. We have to remember that, by denying the use of any word, whatever that word was used for by previous generations not only denies to ourselves the present and the future but also denies the existence of our past and our ancestors overcoming their failures as well their achievements. This only constitutes the worst mistake as we move into the future, because future generations will be denied their ancestors' histories, and creating ignorance for all, just because a small group made us afraid of calling things the way they are and because they imposed their arbitrary rules of political correctness.

ACKNOWLEDGEMENTS

I am a very lucky man because I have a great group of people by my side that I not only consider my friends but also who are the most capable, sacrificing professionals equal to the ones I've risked my life with over the past 50 years in their dedication and values. This group has made possible the publication of this book. To them, with all my heart today, I give the best of my love, gratitude, and sincerest thanks to every one of these fantastic warriors.

In order of seniority, I would especially like to thank O'Brien: a great friend, a great individual with extraordinary values. Thank you for your contributions you have made in many different ways to this project, as well as that beautiful letter you decided to write in my behalf. I know for a fact you have never done that before for anyone.

To my right arm and great friend, Tad Atkinson: for your dedication to every detail in research and many hours of hard work with me, never hesitating to sacrifice even your personal and private family time in order to make this happen.

To Steve Weese: thank you for the splendid artwork on the front and back covers of the book, and many other pieces of computer and graphic work as well professional enhancement of photos to improve the quality of the book.

To Carlos Mota: my thanks for your dedication and multiple contributions and sacrifices you have made in order to make this happen.

To Gervasin Neto: for your constant loyalty and many hours standing on your feet or hiding between cars in order to maintain our security with the group of people you've coordinated to watch our backs, continually keeping us informed of any suspicious activity that occurs in our surroundings.

To Chopin: for your great companionship, loyalty, and support for the last 50 years with me in our fight for freedom and that beautiful, generous letter you wrote in behalf of the project.

To our editor, Jen Poiry-Prough: who managed to make this book as easy to read, using her magic touch to polish this piece of coal and bring to you, the readers, what I consider to be a very rare diamond. It makes all of us very proud to be involved in this project. Your professionalism, vast knowledge, and dedication, has made this book a great piece for future generations.

To Hui Xu (Yo Ko), our latest addition to the team of Christian warriors, thank you for the support which has entirely made this book possible.

To all of you, my friends who remain in the shadows, who contributed in one way or another in making this book and help me to bring the truth to the public, you have given the best of yourselves, putting forth your best effort to educate future generations. God bless you all. I embrace you as the Christian warriors that you all are.

Dr. Julio Antonio del Mármol

Printed in the United States
By Bookmasters